COME TO THE FEAST OF BLESSINGS

AND DISCOVER GOD AS THE LIFE OF THE PARTY!

Copyright © 2023 by Pedro C. Moreno

All rights reserved. Printed and published in the United States of America.

No part of this book may be used or reproduced without written permission.

Front and back cover by Angie at pro_ebookcovers at Fiverr.com

Photos and paintings for front and back cover, Copyright © 2023 by Pedro C. Moreno

First Print: April 2023

To Rael, my beloved partner in mission, and in life.

Appreciation

My heartfelt gratitude to my dear friend Gavin for providing detailed edits for this book. Much appreciated.

To Mark, for his feedback, uplifting comments and daily encouragement and blessings. To Rob, who I know cares about me, and stands with me at all times. Chip, your love and care means a lot to me brother. And Mike (you all know who you are!) for walking with me during a particularly difficult period of my life. I love you brothers!

To my sister Reina, and my brother Miguel Angel, who have always given me their unconditional love and support, and have helped me shape into the man that I am today.

To my kids, Peter and his wife Kyra, Jessica, and Daniel, my joy and my delight. I am so proud of you, and I love you very much. To my Mamilu and my Papi, thank you.

To my beautiful wife Rael, who loves and edifies me every day, and with whom I have the privilege and joy of doing mission, in the midst of the feast. I love you so much baby!

None of this would be possible without the love and life that Jesus Christ gives me every day. Thank you, Lover of my soul.

Table of Contents	Page
Dedication	2
Appreciation	3
Introduction	8

SECTION 1: PEACE WITH GOD

From Hating God to Being Madly in Love with Him	10
From Discipline to Delight	14
From abandoned by my father to abandoned to my father	17
From Having to Do to Getting to Do	19
From Fatherless to Son of God	22
From Earth to Mars and Beyond	25
From Discouragement to Soaring in the Heavens	28
From Religious Boredom to the God of Creation	32
From a Trivialized Day to a God-filled Day	35
From the God of the Church to the God of the Whole World	38
From Youthful Faith to Mature Faith	41
From Cleaning Church Bathrooms to Home Bathrooms	44
From Sterile Existence to Fulfilled Life	47

From a Minority Complex to Leading the Majority	50
From Irrelevant Message to Life-Giving Offer	53
From Tasteless to Being Salt and Light	57
From Church-centered to Kingdom-centered	60
From Shortsightedness to Long Term Vision	63
From Glass Ceiling to Sky is the Limit	66
From Limited Creation to Magnificent Cosmos	69
From Waiting to Die to Living Fully	72
From Things Above to Things Everywhere	75
From Discouragement to Vision	78
From Fragmentation to Integration	82

SECTION 2: PEACE WITH YOURSELF

From Self-hatred to Loving Myself	85
From Inadequacy to becoming a Painter	88
From Famidolatry to Wholesome Life	91
From A Small Town to Downtown D.C.	94
From an Adobe House to the White House	97
From fear of planes to visiting 68 countries on all continents	100
From small world to seeing the world	103

From Fear of Death to Abundant Life	106
From Making Things Happen to Living in Grace	108
From Lack of Self-Management to Managing Complex Operations	111
From Emotionally Deprived to Crying Like a Baby	114
From Loneliness to Companionship	117
From Not Knowing Jesus to Being Known by Him	121
From Either Or to Both and All	124
From Abstinence to Self-Control	127
From Five-Fold to Infinite-Fold	131
From Potted to Planted	135
From Loud Dislike to Quiet Admiration	138
From a Minority Complex to Leading the Majority	140
From Loving Just Hymns to Loving Clean Floors	143
From Overemphasis to Delicate Balance	147
From Black and White to Multicolor Existence	151

SECTION 3: PEACE WITH OTHERS

From Guilty Feeling to Pure Fun	154
From Emotionally Deprived to Passionate Lover	157
From Feeling Shame to Extending Empathy	159

From Old School to the Fletcher School	162
From Loner to Team Player	164
From Pankration to Jiu Jitsu	167
From Losing her Degree to Finding Life	171
From Hopeless Observers to Active Change Agents	174
From Non-Essential to Essential	177
From Squatting to Bowing in Prayer	181
From Pretending to Authenticity	184
From Removing to Renewing Our Minds	187
From Poor Example to Godly Testimony	190
From Otherworldly to a Land of Milk and Honey	193
From Ambivalent Christians to World Changers	197
From One-Dimensional to a Multi-Dimensional Life	200
From Our Timing to His Timing	203
From Mediocrity to Excellent Carpenter	206
From Equal to More Equal than Others (The Family)	210
From Witnessing to Embodying Jesus	214
From Time-Constrained to the Fullness of Time	217

About the Author 221

Introduction

For the longest time I have had issues with relationships. I did not like God the Father, whom I thought of as vengeful and distant. I did not like myself, I felt like damaged goods. And I did not like others, I thought the world was against me.

Even decades after becoming a Christian, I still had these issues. I had the wrong idea of who God really is. Jesus and the Holy Spirit were OK, but not God the Father. I was stuck in the Old Testament. My self-image got better after being born again, but I kept doing things I knew I should not, and I could not live a holy life. I started getting closer to people, but I did not have enough love for them, not even for myself.

All that changed when I finally understood and experienced the fact that God loves me unconditionally, that He is good, all the time, and that Jesus wants to be very close to me. I was able to receive His love for me, and thus love myself. And the more I loved myself, the more I could love others, as myself. I made peace with God, peace with myself, and peace with others.

I went from sinner to saint. And I want to share these meditations with you, of how that happened. My prayer is that it will happen to you too.

Not only does God love us, but He *IS* love. And because He is love He lives in an eternal love feast. No wonder Jesus started His ministry and miracles at a wedding, every communion time is a feast, and the consummation of all things will happen at the marriage feast of the Lamb and His church, which will go on throughout eternity.

So, enter in, it is Feast Time!

From Hating God to Being Madly in Love with Him

I hated God. The Father. Even when I became a Christian. I liked Jesus, He was kind and approachable. And I got along well with the Holy Spirit. He has a tender way of communicating.

But God, the Father, who in the Old Testament was killing men, women, children, even animals, for reasons such as eating the wrong food, carrying something the wrong way, or just plain disobedience, no, I wanted nothing to do with Him.

Maybe it was also a reflection of my relationship with my earthly father. Or lack thereof. I never really had a relationship with him. And the times I remember him were, for example, when he was staring at me (he had a scary stare, just like me), or somehow displeased. I only have one good memory of him, when at a party he picked me up and carried me on his shoulders dancing around the room. That was it. And I hold on to that memory.

Back to God the Father. I thought He really had a temper problem. And I was careful not to disobey too much. I did not want to be fried on the spot. Maybe He was right. Maybe the things that people did in those days warranted the death penalty. I don't know. All I know is that if God had to kill every disobedient person today we would all be gone.

But I judged Him. And resented Him. And held a grudge toward Him. Thankfully He was gracious enough, and let me have a bad attitude toward Him, for a long time, and stay alive.

Actually, it took a couple of decades, as a Christian. I was unable to relate to God the Father. I had blamed not only my earthly father, but God the Father, for the pain I lived through in my childhood, the loneliness, the scarcity, the abandonment.

Well, one day I decided to take matters into my own hands. I was tired of the struggle. I was just waking up, and I said: God, in a few minutes I will forgive you. I waited, in case lighting was on its way. Or the earth would part and swallow me.

Since nothing horrific was happening I said: God, I forgive you. All I felt was a ton of bricks falling off my shoulders. And then I looked up, and in my imagination I saw God the Father, sitting, not on a throne, but on a couch. Looking at me, extending His arms toward me, with a welcoming smile on His face.

I did not know what to do. I looked around, looked back at Him, raised my arms, and I ran toward Him and we both embraced. One of the best experiences of my life.

So, yes, now I love God the Father. My Daddy God. My Abba. I still don't understand many things that happened in the past. All I know is that Jesus made a way for me to know the Father. And now I know that His heart is good. That He is good. All the time.

Matthew 7:11

If you, then, though you are evil, know how to give good gifts to your children, how much more will your Father in heaven give good gifts to those who ask him! NIV

From Discipline to Delight

What do you feel when someone tells you to be disciplined? Or when you tell yourself: I have to have more discipline?

Not a nice feeling, ah? Not the kind of feeling that puts a spring in your step. On the contrary, maybe you feel condemned, ashamed, or guilty.

And then we expect people to come closer to Jesus because of discipline. Or by keeping spiritual disciplines. Or just beating themselves over the head until they get discipline.

How is that working out for you?

It did not work out for me. I tried the discipline thing for a long time as a Christian. It just made things worse, and I felt terrible.

Then I heard about an interview with an Olympic

athlete. The reporter told him: you must have a lot of discipline to get up at 5 am every day and go practice.

The athlete was surprised by the assumption. Quite the opposite, he said. If I tried to do this because of discipline I would have given up a long time ago.

I get up early, he said, because I love what I do. Because I delight in what I do.

So, is it easier to get closer to Jesus because you have the discipline to do so? Or because you love Him and delight in Him?

I've given up on discipline. And I have embraced love and delight. Jesus is so loving and delightful, that I want to know Him better, I desire to come closer to Him, I crave His company and presence. And that is where true discipleship is born.

Song of Solomon 7:10

"I am my beloved's, and his desire is for me. NASB

From abandoned by my father to abandoned to my father

I was taking a class at church one day. And the leader asked: what is your word, in terms of something that causes you pain?

And I blurted out, abandonment.

It was the first time I remember saying that word out loud. Certainly the first time I used it to define something that deep about myself.

I felt kind of embarrassed to say it. And of course I did not want to make my father look bad.

But, it was time to confront reality. Face the pain. Be real about what was ailing me.

To his credit, my father did everything he could or knew to do for me. I don't blame him. Anymore. When he was young he was also abandoned by his own father.

The class helped me understand that abandonment has different meanings. Yes, one of them is the one by which you are left alone. And I was. And I suffered for it.

But there is another meaning. It came to me as a revelation. I thought, well if I am abandoned, I might as well make the most of it.

So, I abandoned myself to my Abba Father. Yes, He is trustworthy, and He will never leave me or forsake me.

Reckless abandon is how I would call it. Totally surrendered to my Daddy God. It is the best kind of abandonment.

Hebrews 13:5
For God has said,
"I will never fail you. I will never abandon you." NLT

From Having to Do to Getting to Do

I remember the message at church in Boston, in Miami, in Virginia. Presbyterian, Charismatic, Bible Church, it was all the same:

You need to give more money to the church. You need to serve at the church more. You need to go on missions, more. You need to read your Bible more. You need to pray more. You need to be a better Christian.

I felt I did not measure up. I was always falling short. Even if I did some or many of these things, the killer-word was always there — more. Nothing was enough.

So I gave up. I was bored reading the Bible. Prayer would put me to sleep. Sometimes I would give money, sometimes not. It did not matter; I was falling short anyway. Why bother.

I was lost in that wilderness for a while. Befuddled.

Bewildered. Confused. Certainly demotivated. And yes, just sinning, one way or the other. Uphill battle.

Then grace happened. I started hearing more about God's grace. About His unconditional love. I became part of a community where vulnerability and love were paramount. I went to a class on grace, and my life started to change.

At that time I heard that the pastor of a large and solid church in Virginia had told all his leaders that if people did not give anything to the church, if they did not pray, if they did not read the Bible, if they did not attend church anymore, God would still love them totally, no matter what.

His leaders were alarmed, and told him that this may be true, but not to tell everyone or attendance would go down and the offerings would shrink.

Au contraire my friends, at least in my case. When I finally was able to dare to accept all this, to internalize all these truths, to overcome major mental obstacles formed through many years at church, and to really believe them, the total opposite happened.

I got to read my Bible. I was excited to put a little pillow on the floor by my bed, and pray every day. I started giving more consistently to the church. I got to go on mission. And yes, I wanted to live a holy life, not because I had to, but because the Holy Spirit inhabits me and loves me.

Mark 2:27
Then he said to them, the Sabbath was made for man, not man for the Sabbath. NIV

From Fatherless to Son of God

One of the earliest memories of my childhood is that of my father standing at the door. Suitcase in hand. Leaving.

Leaving, not just for a while. But leaving for good. In fact, we did not see him again for about 10 years. He had formed a new family -- elsewhere.

I was 5 or so at the time. Sometimes I would see my friends play with their fathers. And call them daddy. I did not have that opportunity.

My brother and I swallowed hard, and promised ourselves not to be hurt again. We would be tough. No emotions allowed. Well, the emotion I allowed in my life was anger. That was it. No warm and fuzzy stuff.

He became special operations military. Me, a lawyer. My sister allowed herself to feel. And it was tough for her. She became a teacher.

As a result, I could not relate to God the Father. Even once I became a Christian. It was hard for me to understand the concept of a good and caring father. I thought father meant distant, judgmental, punishing.

One day, I was playing with my kids. We would go places, the pool, Chuck E. Cheese, the hammock, running around Wal-Mart. And then in the evening, at bedtime, we would sing songs and pray.

And it occurred to me, what if God is a good father? Like me? Who loves and cares for His kids? It sounded a bit sacrilegious. How could I compare God to myself?

Well, it worked. Jesus works in mysterious ways. I ended up understanding, deeply, that God is a good Father all the time. In some ways just like me. Only a million times better, of course.

Now I even call Him Daddy God. And it feels good.

Psalms 2:7

I will proclaim the LORD's decree: He said to me, "You are my son; today I have become your father." New International Version

From Earth to Mars and Beyond

The Bible shows clearly that human beings are the summit of the creation. God made humans last (on the sixth day) and then He rested. He made them in His own image and put them over His creation (animals, plants, and the world in general). As such, we are not just the best that God has created on earth, but the best of the whole universe. And, if God has created the universe, then He placed value on all of it. As the summit of God's creation and as heirs of everything that God has created (Ro.8:17, James 2:5, NAS) we not only have the privilege, but the responsibility to explore our universe.

Obviously there are technological and financial limitations, and we risk losing human lives. But, then again, when were those limitations and risks absent, even in less significant initiatives?

Some young people reason that there is nothing really worth dying for. I would ask them, is there anything worth living for?

Romans 12 instructs us to be "transformed by the renewing of our minds" (v.2, NAS). If we want to make headways in space exploration our existing technology and resources are not enough. We must use our minds creatively. But not only that, we must access the mind of Christ. The Bible tells us that "we have the mind of Christ" (1 Cor. 2:16). Moreover, Jeremiah 33:3 states: "Call to Me, and I will answer you, and I will tell you great and mighty things, which you (some translations say "no one") do not know" (NAS).

In any case, it is clear that we as Christians bear greater responsibility here on earth, and the physical universe, especially if the end of the world doesn't come anytime soon as many are predicting today. Our task continues to be that of faithfulness at work, with family, our nation, studies, leisure and self-renewal as we also pray for and help in pointing people to Christ.

Let us not separate our physical from our spiritual lives. Let us not consider insignificant what may be important to God. Let us consecrate ourselves to a total and integrated Christian life. May our sanctification not only result in individual and family betterment, but also in the transformation of our society and our world so that in the end it will become an inheritance worth leaving to our children.

As we earnestly work for the good of everyone, let us cry out with a longing, "Maranatha! Come Lord Jesus!" While with the same excitement we affirm, "May your kingdom come, on earth as it is in Heaven!"

Matthew 6:9-13

Our Father in heaven, Hallowed be Your name. Your kingdom come. Your will be done on earth as it is in heaven. Give us this day our daily bread. And forgive us our debts, as we forgive our debtors. And do not lead us into temptation, but deliver us from the evil one. For Yours is the kingdom and the power and the glory forever. Amen. NKJV

From Discouragement to Soaring in the Heavens

Could it be that humanity is still in its infancy, at best in its adolescence? I remember talking to a Vatican Nuncio (the Pope's Ambassador). He was convinced that humanity was only in its early days. A quick glance at the injustice, brutality, poverty, discrimination, and conflicts in the world would convince us that humanity has certainly not reached its maturity. We cannot afford to become discouraged and give in to a sense of exhaustion.

It is obvious that we as humans will not be able to cause the calf to lie down with the young lion, or "the nursing child" to play "by the hole of the cobra," or to inspire all men to "hammer their swords into plowshares," as Isaiah describes. This will only be accomplished when Christ Himself comes to rule in His Kingdom. However, the sheer quality and amount of resources God has given us do not allow for any excuse to be paralyzed in the face of mounting moral degradation, corruption, and a sense of hopelessness among our people.

Does God need help in Heaven? Is Jesus Christ lonely and impatient (as some contemporary songs suggest) waiting for His Bride to come to Him? Is the situation on earth so desperate and hopeless as to paralyze us at the bus stop waiting for Jesus to come back?

Sometimes we all have these thoughts and feel that way. I would love to go to Heaven -- today! There is nothing more exciting than Paradise, nothing that captures my imagination so forcefully and joyfully than the thought of spending eternity with God. Hugging Jesus day and night. Celebrating the Feast of the Lamb with the whole cloud of witnesses, in a new and imperishable body, with New Wine, for ever and ever.

All the joys, riches, and glory on earth pale, by far, with what Heaven must be like. For me, as with the Apostle Paul, "to die is gain" (Phil. 1:21 NAS). However, as the Apostle Paul also said, "to live [here on earth] is Christ!" And life in Christ is not just mere survival, but life abundant! Paul also says that "to live on in the flesh" means "fruitful labor" for others' sake (Phil. 1:22, 24).

I cannot wait to go to Heaven. But Heaven can wait. God is not desperate for our help or company. Heaven does not need improvement. If we move one finger trying to help God in Heaven, we will ruin it. Heaven is perfect. Heaven was never corrupted or taken by the devil.

The battle that Jesus Christ fought and won was not over Heaven, but over our souls, over the earth.

In addition to finding God in everything that we do and doing everything as an act of prayer, as an act of worship unto Him, we need ideas and pursuits powerful enough to reignite the hearts and minds of Christians and the rest of society.

What inspires you to go beyond yourself, to get over your own limitations, to forget about pleasing your stomach, and reach for something bigger than your fears, your comfort, your life? What other ideas and pursuits can you think of, big enough to capture our imagination?

Psalm 8:3-4

When I consider your heavens, the work of your fingers, the moon and the stars, which you have set in place, what is mankind that you are mindful of them, human beings that you care for them? NIV

From Religious Boredom to the God of Creation

Let us take the matter of prayer. The Bible does not specifically say how frequently we should pray, for how long at a time, or at what time of the day.

Daniel prayed three times a day. David prayed in the morning. Our Lord Jesus Christ prayed sometimes in the morning, sometimes at night, and most likely at other times as well.

Moreover, Paul instructs us to "pray without ceasing" (1 Thes. 5:17, NAS). Obviously, he did not mean for us to abandon everything, become hermits, and pray day and night (though some have attempted to do so).

In fact, my Bible's heading for that passage (though it is not part of Scripture, but clarifies it anyway) is "Instruction for Holy Living." Thus, we do not cease to pray even as we carry out our daily routines and activities.

And of course those activities, as a result of our praying without ceasing (that is our awareness that everything that we do should be done unto the Lord) ought to be honest, excellent, and legitimate.

Later in that passage the Apostle Paul does suggest that all these instructions, including praying without ceasing, are the way God "sanctifies us entirely" and how our "spirit and soul and body" are "preserved complete, without blame" unto the Lord (v. 23).

Our Lord, thus, is not interested only about our spirit and our spiritual lives, but our minds, our emotions, our bodies, the whole of our being. The Bible would not command us to do something that we are unable to do -- such as praying at the expense of everything else in our lives.

Additionally, and we must be honest about this, once in a while, or for a season, devotional times are plain boring! No matter how much we sit or kneel down and tighten our eyes trying to make connection with God, we get nothing out of it, except to fall asleep.

We read the Scriptures here and there, buy study guides, etc. but get little or no insight from God.

On the other hand, a conversation at work, a letter from one of our relatives, a bike ride, something our spouse or one of our children said, sinks into our heart, revealing more of God to us than some of our devotionals (which can easily become routines or traditions), and making our day, our week, and even our season.

Psalm 96:11-12
Let the heavens rejoice, let the earth be glad; let the sea resound, and all that is in it. Let the fields be jubilant, and everything in them; let all the trees of the forest sing for joy.
NIV

From a Trivialized Day to a God-filled Day

I enjoy attending church, I give my tithe gladly, I believe in the importance of daily prayer and Bible reading, and I share the Gospel whenever there is an opportunity.

Sometimes I have even carried my printed testimony in my wallet, Christian pins on my lapel and shared my faith openly in airplanes, restaurants, meetings, etc.

But to say that my spiritual life is confined to my devotionals and church meetings would be simply ridiculous. Most of my day (the part in which I feel most productive during the daytime) and most of my life, are usually spent on working, eating, commuting etc.

If those activities do not have any relevance to my spiritual life, or any connection with God, then what a waste of my time and life!

Who would want to spend more than 95% of their lives in unimportant, unspiritual, insignificant activities that have nothing to do with God? Or, things that are considered second rate in importance in God's sight?

On the other hand, if daily devotionals, attending church meetings, and evangelizing is so important; if to be really spiritual and please God we should do more and more of these activities, then why not quit our jobs, quit our families, quit our schools, and devote ourselves to such activities all day, for the rest of our lives?

Is this what God intends for all of us to do? The truth is, our work is our prayer. Our whole day and very life is an act of worship unto the Lord. William Diaehl suggests that if our faith is not relevant to our work and our daily routine, then we must have trivialized it "for something that has no relevance to those places where we spend most of our time cannot, after all, be very important."
I firmly believe in the importance of church attendance, in the essential value of quiet times with God, in the

irreplaceable food that comes from the study of God's Word (the Bible), fasting, and evangelism, etc. All I am trying to do here is to put things in proper perspective.

Joshua 24:15

But if serving the LORD seems undesirable to you, then choose for yourselves this day whom you will serve, whether the gods your ancestors served beyond the Euphrates, or the gods of the Amorites, in whose land you are living. But as for me and my household, we will serve the LORD. NIV

From the God of the Church to the God of the Whole World

On the question of our finances, I recently heard a Christian leader say over the radio "First give your tithe to God, then follow your passion about how to spend the rest of your money." Scripture, however, provides a different perspective.

It is not just our tithe that is given to God. In Romans 13, the Apostle Paul after pointing out that "it is necessary to submit to the authorities" states that "[t]his is also why you pay taxes, for the authorities are God's servants, who give their full time to governing" (v. 6, NIV).

And then Paul insists "[g]ive everyone what you owe him: If you owe taxes, pay taxes; if revenue, then revenue..." (v. 7).

On this same matter, when our Lord Jesus Christ was questioned about whether it was "right to pay taxes to Caesar," He clearly responded "Give to Caesar [the state] what is Caesar's" (Mt. 22:17, 21, NIV).

Regarding our family expenses, the Bible commands us to take care of our family or we have "denied the faith" and are "worse than an unbeliever" (1 Tim. 5;8, NIV).

Thus, we are giving to God not just when we bring the tithe to the church, but also when we pay our taxes, take care of our family, pay for school, vacation, or any other legitimate activity (whatever is not sinful).

Not just the tithe but all of our money belongs to God.

Now, there may be situations when, for a temporary period, we may have to devote more time to one of these jurisdictions demanding urgent attention. For example, if a member of our family is in trouble, then we may have to take days off from work or even leave our studies aside for a while until we can solve the problem.

Equally, if our church or work is going through a transition and they need extra hours from us, we may have to cut down on the time spent with our families in order to take care of these urgent tasks.

However, we should never let such responses to these crises and emergencies become permanent modes of operation.

Psalm 97:1
The Lord reigns, let the earth be glad; let the distant shores rejoice. New International Version

From Youthful Faith to Mature Faith

I remember when I was a single student, living in Boston, Massachusetts. I was a nonbeliever, until some Christian families and a minister to international students reached out to me and invited me into their homes. As I observed them eating, talking to each other, and smiling, I realized they had something I didn't. And I wanted it. No one preached the Gospel to me with words. They lived the Gospel, befriending me, loving me.

I began asking questions. Who are you? Why do you do this? Why are you so happy? As a result, I became a Christian, inside the minister's car, right at the subway stop on a cold New England night.

That moment initiated a new stage in my life. For sure, this stage has been the most exciting and rewarding, but also one filled with challenges. At that time, in the midst of my "honeymoon" with the Lord, I used to pray 2 or 3 hours a day, read my Bible frequently, attended church 4 or 5 times a week, and evangelized on the streets and wherever else.

I was constantly in fellowship with other believers, and felt a mountain-top joy. Then life started to change. Family, mortgage, additional responsibilities at work, travelling, further education, etc., etc., etc. As I reflected on my busy life, without all that time for prayer, Bible study and church, I started feeling condemned, guilty, and separated from God. But then I caught myself and realized that my life had in fact changed.

My relationship with the Lord had also changed and had matured. I do not need to feel at the top of the mountain -- in fact many times I feel in the deep valley -- to be close to the Lord. Instead, the Lord oftentimes meets us at the bottom of the pit -as He did with Jonah in the fish's belly.

Rather than expecting the Lord to touch me while I jump up and down with my friends in joy (which I do not have much time to do anymore), the Lord touches me now as I change a dirty diaper and clean every interstice in my child's skin, so that their transcendent life is not ruined by a rash!

Rather than trying to regurgitate the good old spiritual life of a mostly worry-free student with plenty of spare time, I now feel the sobering yet uplifting presence of the Lord as I am diligent at work and faithful to my wife.

So, where does God fit into our daily schedule? Everywhere.

Psalm 139:7-10
Where can I go from your Spirit? Where can I flee from your presence? If I go up to the heavens, you are there; if I make my bed in the depths, you are there. If I rise on the wings of the dawn, if I settle on the far side of the sea, even there your hand will guide me, your right hand will hold me fast. NIV

From Cleaning Church Bathrooms to Home Bathrooms

Related to the question of church activities, the idea that God is found only in the church building is of course wrong. It was true for the Old Testament, when God appeared in the Tabernacle and later inhabited the Holy of Holies at the physical Temple.

But not anymore. Jesus Christ has given us the Holy Spirit to live inside each one of us. Therefore, the Church, the universal church, is manifested in us and through us individually as well as collectively, and is present wherever Christians happen to be.

Now, I've heard pastors say "if you want to give something to the Lord, come and teach Sunday school, help with the sound equipment, clean the church bathrooms."

So, cleaning the church bathrooms can amount to "giving to God" but not cleaning our home's bathrooms. Doing technical work with church equipment is "giving to God" but not doing technical work at our workplace. Teaching Sunday school is "giving to God" but not forming the minds and hearts of our young people in our public schools. What are we talking about?

The "ordinary," the "routine," the "monotonous" is something that we must bear, even grudgingly, hoping that at some point, we will be able to do something else in or with the church. Ironically, when finally offered the opportunity to go to the mission field, many Christians decline because they do not really want to leave their comfort-zone and face the hardships of the unknown. Or because others will not support them.

In the meantime, the next best thing we can do is give as much money as we can to the church so others can go do the really important and spiritual work.
Thus goes on our life, in the midst of confusion, guilt, and insecurity, never measuring up to the expectations of what a "truly spiritual life" should really be or what it means to be "better disciples" and "better Christians."

However, isn't this "boring," "non-transcendent," "second-class," and "routine" life, the one that in fact makes possible any societal life at all? Aren't these "predictable" people giving stability to society and continuity to our human endeavors?

Imagine if we were all missionaries, or itinerant artists. Aren't these "monotonous" tasks producing the food, the medical care, the law and order necessary for us to exist in society?

Matthew 6:26
Look at the birds of the air; they do not sow or reap or store away in barns, and yet your heavenly Father feeds them. Are you not much more valuable than they? NIV

From Sterile Existence to Fulfilled Life

Let us all remember and remind each other who we are in Christ: a royal priesthood, a chosen people, ambassadors of Christ, eternal beings, endowed with the mind of Christ, with access to the most powerful weapons (spiritual ones), bought by the blood of the Lamb, heirs and summit of all creation, entrusted with the most exciting mission on earth -- to transform our world -- and empowered by the Holy Spirit who lives inside of us.

Why then is it that we frequently get bogged down by questions such as: Have you prayed enough this morning? Are you happy with how many people you have evangelized in the past months? Do you feel that your Bible study time is at the level it should be? Are you doing enough for your church?

Do these questions cause a sense of uneasiness in you? Outright guilt, perhaps? If you are a normal American, you spend most of your day working, eating, sleeping, commuting and doing the daily routines of life.

In fact, someone has calculated that in a life-span of 70 years your life will most likely be spent as follows: 24 years sleeping, 11 years working, 8 years playing, 6 years eating, 5 years travelling (commuting), 4 years talking, 3 years suffering from illnesses, 3 years reading, and 3 years learning.

That would take a total of 67 years. Now, if you attended all church services and prayed for 15 minutes a day, by the end of your life you would have "given to God" only a little more than 2 years of your time. For a grand total of 70 years.

It is true that the average Christian in America, on a typical week, spends more time in his or her morning personal hygiene than in prayer, Bible study, and church attendance combined.

And when it comes to working, commuting or eating, the gap is much greater.

However, instead of feeling guilty all over again about it, I think it is high time to ask: so what?

And not only that but, what is the truth of the matter? If God were only found in prayer, Bible study, and at the church building, and since we do not do those things all or even a substantial part of the time, how utterly impoverished, how limited, how spiritually sterile and miserable our lives would be.

Others, on the other extreme, have conveniently boxed God into a 1-hour (2 hours for the really "committed") package for Sunday morning, and a 15 to 30 minute daily devotional. Aside from that, their lives are theirs to live as they see fit.

1 Corinthians 10:31
So whether you eat or drink or whatever you do, do it all for the glory of God. NIV

From a Minority Complex to Leading the Majority

A Christian executive once told me that it would be good if the "pagans" would leave us alone. He suggested that if we Christians could keep "a couple of states" where we would develop our communities according to Christian principles, the "pagans" could take the rest of the country. This could be called the Christian reservation mentality.

Feeling alienated, and in many cases, hopeless about the course of events in this world, many Christians find comfort thinking about retreating, or the end of this world and life in the world after.

While this notion could be considered biblical and we certainly see examples of this throughout scripture, of people of God waiting for their final deliverance -- I believe that we have brought this mentality too far.

The consequences of this minority mentality, which manifests itself in isolation, alienation, and irrelevance are deadly not only to the community at large but to Christians themselves.

However, we Christians do not have to become, and in fact are not, a minority.

Let us take the question of distinctiveness. Obviously Christians are different from the rest of society, chiefly because of the fact that they have been redeemed by the Savior of the world.

But, if we analyze our lives and the lives of others closely, we will realize that we as Christians are not that different from the rest of society. We still work, raise our children, go to school, play sports, and so on. In fact, most of what we do for most of our lives as humans -- eating, sleeping, commuting, etc. -- is no different from anybody else's.

Matthew 22:35-40
One of them, an expert in the law, tested him with this question: "Teacher, which is the greatest commandment in the Law?" Jesus replied: "'Love the Lord your God with all

your heart and with all your soul and with all your mind. This is the first and greatest commandment. And the second is like it: 'Love your neighbor as yourself.' All the Law and the Prophets hang on these two commandments." NIV

From Irrelevant Message to Life-Giving Offer

On the point of categorical representation or group identity, we must go back to the Bible. It is true that Jesus Christ said "he who is not with Me is against Me" (Luke 11:23, NAS), thus we could partially explain our distrust for those not in the community of faith.

However, in a passage that we tend to overlook, Jesus Christ also said that "...he who is not against you is for you" (Luke 9:50, NAS). That means that we could find a common purpose, even with non-believers. That means that non-believers are also capable of doing good.

Moreover, that also means that truth, wherever it is found, proceeds from and belongs to God. It was a Christian missionary to India, William Carey, who first translated and published the great Indian philosophical and religious classics into English.

These classics were of course not "Christian," but contained much wisdom and insight that could only come from that "eternity in their heart" (Ecc. 3:11, NAS) with which God has endowed all His creatures.

Furthermore, the Bible, in Romans 13 states that authorities are "ministers of God." This verse implies that authorities do not necessarily have to be Christian in order to be ministers of God.

Even our contemporary authorities at the national level (President, Congress, the Courts), are implementing policies, and handing down decisions that for the most part have our (explicit or tacit) support.

We may disagree strongly with individual executive and court decisions, but by-and-large we have not reached the point where it would be justifiable to write off our government, our laws, and our institutions, regardless of who is in power.

On the other hand, many self-identified Christian authorities did not fulfill the expectations that many Christians had of them as they discharged their duties.

Concerning the disinterest of society for the Christian message, it is true that as commonly presented, it has become largely irrelevant to society. In fact, because of its contents (limited to the "religious/evangelistic" with disregard for every other aspect of life) it has become irrelevant to Christians themselves.

Why would anybody care about a message that concentrates solely or mainly in life after death? A message that is so wrapped up in religious jargon that it becomes unintelligible? A message that purports to be global in its scope and applicable to all but in practice reveals a very narrow focus, that of "saving souls" -- forgetting about the bodies, the minds, and the emotions of people?

Ecclesiastes 3:11
He has made everything beautiful in its time. He has also set

eternity in the human heart; yet no one can fathom what God has done from beginning to end. NIV

From Tasteless to Being Salt and Light

To be sure, the Lord Jesus Christ also said "In the world, you [will] have tribulation" (John 16:33, NAS).

The Lord Jesus Christ said that if we are struck on one cheek, to give the other. However, in the only instance in the Bible where it is recorded that Christ was struck on the cheek, He demanded an explanation for that kind of action -- "Jesus replied, 'If I was wrong to speak what I did, produce evidence to prove it; if I was right, why strike me?'" (John 18:23, REB).

He did not surrender in false humility. Ultimately of course, Jesus Christ gave the other cheek in a way that none of us could do, by becoming the sin and the curse of the world and dying on the cross. We must discern the times, whether it is appropriate to give the other cheek, or whether it is time to take a stand and resist oppression.

Christians never constituted a majority in the world.

However, that did not prevent the twelve rugged, uneducated, down-to-earth disciples from turning the world upside down.

It did not prevent William Wilberforce from being greatly instrumental in the abolition of slavery in Britain. It did not prevent Martin Luther King from fighting a battle against racial discrimination based on the Bible and the principles enshrined in the Declaration of Independence and the Constitution.

And even if we want to talk only about "committed" Christians, they are supposed to be at least a quarter of the American population. Can we not overcome our mental state of separation, our minority complex, and become the salt and light in this dark world?

I believe with all my heart that we can, and I also believe that the glory of the Lord will fill the whole earth (Psalm 72:19, NAS). Our perspective is global. The Bible is the truth of God, which has been spoken for all people, not just for

Christians. Our God is not one among many, but the God of the universe, Creator of everything that exists.

The command given to us by the Lord Jesus Christ in Matthew 28:18-20 when He said "All authority has been given to Me in heaven and on earth. Go therefore and make disciples of all the nations... teaching them to observe all that I commanded you" has not become obsolete, and does not refer only to "souls" but nations as well. Further, the Lord promises us "Lo, I am with you always..." (NAS). What else do we need?

Matthew 19:26

Jesus looked at them and said, "With man this is impossible, but with God all things are possible." NIV

From Church-centered to Kingdom-centered

It is good that we have an independent and enterprising spirit and that we are not waiting for others to take the initiative. It is a strength for us as individuals and a hallmark of our nation.

But we must also recognize that we need each other, that we are interdependent, and that others need our time, even if that means reducing the amount of time that we spend with our families.

Further, we must be secure enough to humble ourselves and receive help and blessings from others when needed.

At work, we want to succeed, increase our income, and find fulfillment in our professional responsibilities. In doing so, many of us have become workaholics.

The Bible clearly commands us to work. In fact, it is a blessing from the Lord. Even before the fall, Adam worked, tending the garden, naming the animals, etc.

Our Lord Jesus Christ Himself says "My Father is always at his work to this very day, and I, too, am working" (John 5:17, NIV).

Thus, hard work is godly, good and necessary, However, it should not be done at the expense of our family, or used as an excuse for poor church participation.

Church demands for our time, energy, and resources make some feel that in order to be truly spiritual, they have to attend church every night, or as frequently as possible (sometimes several times a week).

They also feel that in order to have their money invested properly, or "given to God," they need to give it to the church, even if that means taking it away from other responsibilities.

Others may think that Christian life is one of contemplation and meditation, falling into false pietism and alienation. On the other extreme, some see church just as a weekend or Sunday morning routine that has nothing to do with the rest of their week.

Luke 17:20-21

Once, on being asked by the Pharisees when the kingdom of God would come, Jesus replied, "The coming of the kingdom of God is not something that can be observed, nor will people say, 'Here it is,' or 'There it is,' because the kingdom of God is in your midst."

From Shortsightedness to Long Term Vision

There is a need to balance the preaching of the "imminent" return of Jesus Christ, and the "rapture" with the understanding that Jesus Christ may tarry.

The last words of the Lord Jesus Christ recorded in the Bible are indeed "Yes, I am coming quickly." (Rev. 22:20).

However, "quickly" has so far meant over 2,000 years.

If we are going to change the world in the economic, political and social realms, as well as the spiritual, we will need to be prepared for the long term.

Just as proper encouragement should be given to church members considering serving in an ecclesiastical ministry (pastors, missionaries, evangelists, etc.), so should the same kind of encouragement be given to members choosing different professions or occupations.

This is especially true of students seeking to confirm their academic vocation.

Every aspect of life can be used for the service of our Lord. We as Christians can give a testimony of diligence, excellence, service, and integrity in everything that we do.

As the Church is composed of all believers, it is present wherever believers carry out their activities, ministering to their neighbor and serving God.

To effectively impact our society requires that we Christians see all areas of society, not just the church, as part of God's Kingdom.

It will also necessitate that our emotions be balanced and enriched by reason; that we see ourselves as ministers of God in all that we do; and that while anticipating Christ's prompt return, we are prepared for the long run.

Acts 1:7

He said to them: "It is not for you to know the times or dates the Father has set by his own authority." NIV

From Glass Ceiling to Sky is the Limit

Why are we here on earth? What did God intend when He created us and placed us on this planet? What is the purpose of our continued existence as the human race?

These questions may never be answered. Or even if the answers were available we may never fully comprehend them with our finite minds.

However, there is no reason why we should not explore some possible answers. In fact, many have already done so and come to different conclusions.

Some of those conclusions have created what I call the Christian glass ceiling. That is, the limitations that Christians have imposed on themselves because of a particular understanding of Scripture.

They emphasize Heaven over the earth, the spirit over the mind and body, church and evangelism over work, science, etc.; and the planet earth over the rest of the universe.

But, let us imagine God at the moment before Creation took place. There He is, in all His eternal and infinite magnificence, beauty, and power.

There is no physical universe as we know it. He then pronounces the words "Let there be light."

And launches the whole universe into existence, with its billions of galaxies, stars, and planets.

Then He picks one of those billions of planets, called earth, and says: "Let us make man in Our image, according to Our likeness; and let them rule... over all the earth" (Gen. 1:26, NAS).

How do you feel about this? Does it move you to worship, perhaps?

Genesis 1:27

So God created mankind in his own image, in the image of God he created them; male and female he created them. NIV

From Limited Creation to Magnificent Cosmos

Some contend that God created humans with the main purpose of bringing them to Heaven. Then the whole universe would be rolled back.

If that is so, why would have God made humans immortal (and apparently the animals and everything else) when He created them and placed them on the earth, not in Heaven?

The facts according to Scripture are these: God created Adam and Eve and made them immortal.

Not only that, but God placed them in the Garden of Eden here on earth, not in Heaven.

That means that God intended for Adam and Eve to live here, on earth, forever.

That also means that not only humans were immortal but possibly also the earth, the sun, and the universe (how exactly, I don't know, but then again, we don't know many things about God).

Death came after Adam and Eve sinned. As Romans 5:12 says "...through one man sin entered into the world, and death through sin..." (NAS).

Sin obviously not only corrupted and brought death to Adam and Eve but also to the universe itself. That is why everything is now deteriorating, going from complex to simple, according to the laws of thermodynamics.

Moreover, if God had intended to create humans with the main purpose of bringing them with Him to Heaven, He would have created humans, and them only.

He did not need to bother creating the whole universe -- unless He had other plans for the universe, which to date we know nothing about.

Isaiah 6:3

And they were calling to one another: "Holy, holy, holy is the Lord Almighty; the whole earth is full of his glory." NIV

From Waiting to Die to Living Fully

The Second Coming of Jesus Christ (and thus the end of the world as we know it), was not conditioned to the full evangelization of the world. At least not in the apostles' minds. As an example, Paul thought that Christ would come back before he died (1 Thes. 4: 15,17).

Also, Christians have been making predictions about the end of the world for centuries, and especially at the end of the first millennium and of course at the end of the second millennium.

Another argument is that these are the "last days" of our world. That is true. But it was also true of the days of the 12 apostles (about 2,000 years ago).

Peter, in explaining the events at Pentecost when he and the other apostles were filled with the Holy Spirit and spoke in different tongues, pointed out that it had already been prophesied by Joel that this would occur in the "last days" (Acts 2:16, 17, NAS).

Others say, yes, but we are "nearer" to the end -- 2,000 years "nearer."

And that is true too. But, so what? What would you think if a 5-year old child or a teenager was talking frequently about his or her "approaching" death?

It is true that after we are born we start getting closer to our death. It is also true that the young person would be 5 years "nearer" to his or her death.

But, so what? What kind of mentality is that? Would we consider that young person's perspective to be a healthy one?

It is possible that somebody will die young (in fact many do). But early death is not guaranteed, in the same way that the Lord and the Bible do not guarantee us (much less give us a date) that our death as the human race, as the world, will take place in "a couple of years" or "months."

The Lord Jesus Christ did say that He was coming back "soon" (Rev. 22:20), but we should know by now (after almost 2,000 years) that the time-span of His "soon" is much longer than our "soon."

Revelation 22:12-21
Look, I am coming soon! NIV

From Things Above to Things Everywhere

Some quote Colossians 3:2 (and similar scriptures), which says: "[s]et you mind on things above, not on the things that are on earth" and conclude that what we do here on earth, such as work, studies, science, etc. is not really important.

What we need to concentrate on is the "things above" the "heavenly things" such as church, evangelism, prayer, etc.

However, the context of this and similar verses lead us to a different conclusion.

Further down, Colossians clarifies the picture when it says in verses 5 and 6: "Therefore consider the members of your earthly body as dead to immorality, impurity, passion, evil desire, and greed, which amounts to idolatry. For it is on account of these things that the wrath of God will come..."

So, what scripture means here by "things that are on earth" is not the arts, science, business, politics, etc. but sin.

Conversely, what scripture means here by instructing us to set our minds on "things above" is not to start looking at the clouds to see which one the Lord is riding on in His Second Coming, or evangelizing all day, or attending church day and night.

But to understand that we have been regenerated, that we must stop sinning, and that we have been enabled to live a holy life in everything that we do.

In any case, the fact is that we (the human race) are still here on earth. And we may continue to be here for another 2,000 years or longer.

No matter how many earthquakes, plagues, and wars the prophets of our time count in making their predictions that the end of the world will happen in the next few years, or even months, one fact remains:

It is not for us "to know times or epochs which the Father has fixed by His own authority" (Acts 1:7, NAS).

Isaiah 55:8-9

"For my thoughts are not your thoughts, neither are your ways my ways," declares the Lord.

"As the heavens are higher than the earth, so are my ways higher than your ways and my thoughts than your thoughts. NIV

From Discouragement to Vision

Not only have we not evangelized the earth in 2,000 years (it should have been sufficient time for us to do so, especially if that is the "real purpose" for our continued stay here on earth), but due to the constant birth rate, rejection and abandonment of the faith, and other factors, it seems that the evangelistic effort may never be exhausted or completed.

Thus, our "real purpose" (to evangelize) if taken as our only "important" activity and the only standard of success for our mission here on earth, could eventually become an exercise in futility, and lead us all to despair. This has already happened for many Christians.

Going back to the question of the Christian glass ceiling, I believe that, as a result of our prevalent theology, we have set at least three glass ceilings against ourselves which are hindering our lives and our societal impact:

First, at the individual level, the glass ceiling is our overemphasis on the importance of the "spirit" at the expense of our body, and especially our mind.

Second, at the collective level, the glass ceiling is our insistence on putting the church, evangelism, and "spiritual disciplines" (such as prayer, Bible reading, etc.) over every other aspect of our lives (work, family, nation, studies, cooking, etc.)

Third, at the global level, we have put the earth and its resources as the limit of our discovery process, our imagination, and our commitment for exploration and have set it over the rest of the universe.

Now, having adopted this theology and these three glass ceilings, we have concluded that we have exhausted (or at least are close to exhausting) whatever was there to explore, know, or experience. At the individual level, knowing that our spirit has been regenerated by Christ, and thinking that our bodies and minds are of no real importance; we are ready (oftentimes eager) to go to the other world.

Collectively, certain evangelists are claiming that for the first time in the history of the world, and counting on existing technology (Internet, satellites, television, airplanes, etc.), we can "get the job done" -- that is evangelize the whole world and then the end will come.

At the global level, we have come to believe that the earth's resources are rapidly depleting, we have grown tired of eating and wasting, and are fed up with consumerism which does not bring the happiness that we expected.

And we are discouraged by the corruption of the political process, the persistence of racial disharmony, and have ultimately concluded that since we have mapped out all continents, visited the undersea, and understood the laws of aerodynamics, there is nothing else to do or explore on this planet.

Isaiah 45:3

I will give you hidden treasures, riches stored in secret places, so that you may know that I am the Lord, the God of Israel, who summons you by name. NIV

From Fragmentation to Integration

If the "things of this world" are not really important, Jesus Christ (the God of the universe) would never have taken up a human body and come into this world physically.

He would never have eaten of the product of this world, he would never have mentioned seeds, and coins, and chickens, in His teachings.

If our spirits are the only things He is interested in, He could have saved us directly from Heaven.

Not only did the God of the universe decide to come in a human body and into this physical existence, but He arguably wasted most of His limited time here on earth. Thirty of His 33 years on earth are spent on unimportant, non-transcendent, insignificant activities such as carpentry work, playing, eating, etc.

He ends up exercising His "ministry" for only 3 years. He missed out big time! Or, did He?

The fact is that all areas of our life are interdependent and interconnected. We are not human beings if we take into account only our spirit.

Our mind and our body are integral and essential parts of our being. We could not function in this world if we did not have all of these acting in unison.

The local church and evangelism would be impossible without the participation of other spheres of life. These satellites, airplanes, television, Internet, etc. that the evangelists are happily using to reach the world with the gospel, once and for all, have not come out of the blue.

In fact, they would have never been invented if the previous generation had despised and minimized science, technology, etc. as some are doing today. For science and technology to be possible we need to build one step at the time, over a long period of time in a historical inter-connection.

This began with basic mathematical and physical calculations, extended to electricity, the transistor, the microchip, the telephone, and now includes the computer, Internet, and artificial intelligence. It was not an easy and shortsighted process. It required centuries of scientific development.

Hebrews 12:1
Therefore, since we are surrounded by such a great cloud of witnesses, let us throw off everything that hinders and the sin that so easily entangles. And let us run with perseverance the race marked out for us. NIV

From Self-hatred to Loving Myself

I am ashamed to admit this, but I used to join others in discrimination. Against the so-called "Indians" in Bolivia, whom we would despise as ignorant, and dirty.

But that was not all. We would also hate the Spaniards, who as colonists we would blame for raping the women and taking all the gold, silver and riches back to Europe.

Then, one day I looked at myself in the mirror. And I recognized that I am a mix of Indian and Spaniard. Which was a hard pill to swallow.

Even worse, it dawned on me that in hating the Spaniards and the Indians, I hated myself. I felt shame.

Thankfully, Jesus Christ provides restorative shame, which is still shame, but not the destructive type that leads to despair.

It is the type that He used to restore me, my self-image, and my view of others. My outlook changed. I saw others with empathy. Because they reminded me of myself. They were me. And I was them.

And then the long process of learning how to love myself began. And how to love others, as myself.

I did not have enough love, even for myself. Much less for others. I could not produce love, fabricate it, or manufacture it. Affection? Yes. Care? Maybe. Possibly even infatuation. But not love.

So, I surrendered. To the love of God. Manifested in Jesus Christ. And His death on the cross. That is true love. That is Agape love -- unconditional love. That is the love I received, and continue to receive every day.

Now that I am able to receive His love, which He pours on me every day, unconditionally, I can love Him back, and love myself. And love others, including the "Indians" and the Spaniards, and everyone else.

1 John 4:19-21

We love because he first loved us. Whoever claims to love God yet hates a brother or sister is a liar. For whoever does not love their brother and sister, whom they have seen, cannot love God, whom they have not seen. And he has given us this command: Anyone who loves God must also love their brother and sister. NIV

From Inadequacy to becoming a Painter

I was young, in middle school, and during art class I decided to paint. One painting. It came out alright. I titled this oil canvas "Boys by the Lake."

Then I felt inadequate. Insecure. The proverbial "I can't even draw a stick figure" syndrome took hold of me. Decades went by. And I forgot all about painting. I became cerebral, calculating, logical.

Visiting a friend of mine some years ago in North Carolina, I saw his watercolors on the wall. I admire him a lot, so I said, "brother, I want to be like you. How can I paint?"

This godly man said: Go to Michael's, and for $35 you can get the whole set of brushes, paints, and watercolor paper. I did, and that same day, by the lake house, I painted my first painting of this season of my life. Titled "Pier by the Lake" (I guess I really like lakes, and water!).

In the next 5 years, 500 plus other paintings followed. Given as a gift to people in 15 countries.

Hotel attendants, colleagues in the office, friends, random people at the grocery store, people at church, and others I had just met, received a painting, as a symbol of God's unconditional love for them.

One lady said, "I'm shocked, it means a lot." Someone else said: "I've never got a painting from anyone," and cried. A pastor even said: "This is the best gift I got since my engagement!"

Now, it is not that the paintings are perfect. They are not. Or that they even have a lot of artistic style in them. They really don't. I am self-taught, and I just want to develop my emotional intelligence while blessing others with my paintings.

I actually humbly consider myself part of the stenographic school of painters. Those who are minimalist in their painting, and leave the interpretation and most of the details to the viewer.

Who, by the grace of Jesus, see something worthwhile in them and get blessed.

1 John 4:19

We love because he first loved us. ESV

From Famidolatry to Wholesome Life

I used to believe that my family was the most important thing after God. Then, in a gradation, came church, then work, etc.

Not anymore. I love my family dearly, and I would do anything for them and to spend even more time with them.

However, I have come to realize that if I am to have a healthy life that will impact the world around me, my family needs to be as important as my church, as valuable as my work, as significant as my nation, as vital as self-renewal, and as needed as my academic pursuits.

I also believe that God is not found only at church. He is also found, indeed, is the head of our family, our workplace, our nation, our school, and all areas of life. That is why we must pursue excellence and give our best in all these areas. And do it simultaneously!

To illustrate the point, let us imagine a 5-spoked wheel. At the hub is the individual in Christ. The 5 spokes are the family, work, church, leisure/self-renewal, and education. The whole wheel represents an individual's life in Christ.

If one of these spokes is weak or missing, then the whole wheel will be weakened and ineffective. Consequently, we will not travel too far.

The over-emphasis on individualism and self-sufficiency in our culture, has created an introspective and nuclear-family oriented attitude. It is a kind of famidolatry.

The Bible does say that "If anyone does not provide for his relatives, and especially for his immediate family, he has denied the faith and is worse than an unbeliever." (1 Tim. 5:8, NIV).

There is no question that we must provide and take care of our families. But that does not mean that we should retreat into our household, make our spouse and children our gods and have little participation in the lives of others.

Because "my wife is my best friend," I do not have an excuse not to cultivate friendships with others. According to statistics, over 90% of all men in America do not have a friend; buddies and partners, yes, but not friends.

The resulting effect is the philosophy of "I do not need you, you should not need me."

Ephesians 4:16
From him the whole body, joined and held together by every supporting ligament, grows and builds itself up in love, as each part does its work. NIV

From A Small Town to Downtown D.C.

I was born and grew up in a small town of 15,000 people called Tupiza, in Bolivia.

At the time there was barely a car on the streets, there were a couple of traffic lights, and people were not in a hurry to go anywhere.

Young people rode their bikes, and older folks walked. The main Plaza was the center of life, whether to see friends, or listen to music and have fun on the weekends.

If you went for a few blocks, you were out of town. Which was nice, since we were surrounded by tall red hills, two intersecting rivers, and lots of fields with trees of every kind, especially figs, apricots, apples, pears, and corn.

I felt safe, people did not bother with locks of any kind, and we all knew each other.

Then came the time to outgrow it. I was restless, I wanted to learn more, to see more of the country, and the world.

My sister who was living in Virginia with her family invited me to come to the U.S. I left in a jiffy, became a Christian shortly after arriving, and ended up working in Washington DC.

DC as we all know is its own animal. If you want to have a friend in DC, says the axiom, get a dog. So I got a dog (and some friends too).

I learned to love the United States while working in the DC area. I became part of the non-profit world advocating for life, family and religious freedom, and later joined the Federal government with a couple of Administrations. I was there, close to the Pentagon, when we were attacked on September 11, which made me love our country all the more.

Through it all, I learned that my small town upbringing instilled life and values that I would need when lost in the maze of the big city. We have a blessed country, governed from the Nation's Capital. But more importantly, we have a big and mighty King, who deserves our gratitude and loyalty.

Daniel 4:17
The decision is announced by messengers, the holy ones declare the verdict, so that the living may know that the Most High is sovereign over all kingdoms on earth and gives them to anyone he wishes and sets over them the lowliest of people. NIV

From an Adobe House to the White House

The door to the Oval office opened, and the President himself ushered my family and I into his presence.

How could this be possible? I remember growing up in an adobe house, in a small town in Bolivia. Yes, the walls were solid and 2 feet wide, we would have bookstands carved out in them. The house was
somewhat spacious, compared to the neighbors, but it still had problems.

The walls would get wet with the rain. The paint would crack, and endless repairs were needed, once again. Over and over. My siblings and I felt a little insecure about the solidity of the foundations.
And I would help put some cement into the holes. Yes, cement, just in case. Keep those walls up.

Fast forward a couple of decades. I was working with a non-profit in Virginia, and I said, I would like to work at the

White House.

Some of my friends thought I was insane. We would ALL like to work at the White House, they said. So, I felt a little unsure about the whole idea.

But, undeterred I started looking into it, and submitted my resume just as a new President was assuming office. It looked like an impossible
task, if only because there were more than a hundred qualified candidates for every position.

Then, a friend from Bolivia shows up visiting Washington D.C. with his family. He asks, "what are you up to these days?" And I say, "I'm trying to get a job at the White House."

And oh miracle of miracles, only Jesus could do something like this. Turns out a friend of my just arrived friend, who had been a pilot in Bolivia, worked at one of the White House offices.

Lo and behold, my resume was passed from hand to hand, and it went up to the decision makers.

I got the call. And the rest, like everything else in Washington, is history.

Mark 10:27
Jesus looked at them and said, "With man this is impossible, but not
with God; all things are possible with God." NIV

From fear of planes to visiting 68 countries on all continents

There I was, at 35,000 feet, cruising on a transatlantic 767, when I started feeling turbulence.

I had felt turbulence before, and every time I did I would start praying. Not just for myself, but for the whole plane. Somehow I felt that if I stopped praying we would all be in trouble.

And I kept praying, though I was tired. I wanted to go to sleep, it was a 7-hour flight. But no, I needed to pray. I must pray. Everyone depends on me.

Somehow I had come to believe that faith is on me, that prayer depends on me, that I must do the work.

Finally, I decided to confront the issue at hand. And confront it head on. Deeply. Like, what would happen if I die right now?

Then I thought of Jesus Christ, who is much bigger and better than me. Able to take care of me. Able to keep the plane flying. Able to take care of everyone. Everywhere. No matter what.

I thought about it for a long moment, and then I finally exhaled. And I thought, oh well, if I die right now, I will go to Heaven.

Because Heaven does not depend on me. I cannot earn it. I cannot pray myself into it. It comes to me as a free gift from God, that I just need to humbly receive.

And somehow my family will be taken care of. And everything will go on.

So, I gave up. And I went to sleep. And ended up visiting 68 countries, on all continents.

Jude 1:24-25
"Now unto him that is able to keep you from falling, and to

present you faultless before the presence of his glory with exceeding joy, to the only wise God our Saviour, be glory and majesty, dominion and power, both now and ever. Amen." KJV

From small world to seeing the world

I was 8 years old or so when I told my friends I wanted to see the world. They looked puzzled and asked: How do you intend to do that if you don't have the money?

At the time I lived in a small town in Bolivia, about 15,000 people. Nice red mountains, two rivers that connected to each other nearby, and lots of space to ride my bike with my friends, for miles, without a worry in the world.

But money was an issue. We did not have much money at all. In fact, my mother was able to get me a bicycle only when I was 11 years old or so, and a tape recorder. That was when she finally got a stable job (that is another story, elsewhere in this book).

So, the idea that I could see the world was ludicrous then.

I was finishing my law degree (tuition is free in the public universities there), and I wanted to go international. So, I went to the Japanese embassy, and then the Italian embassy, and then the American embassy. Looking for scholarships.

Found none. No scholarships. No way out.

Enter Jesus. My sister had become a Christian, gotten married, and moved to the United States. And she and her husband and family helped me navigate an application for summer school.

In the meantime, I was getting involved in every international meeting I could find in Bolivia. That way I would get the global DNA, so to speak, and then hopefully go international.

The day came, when I received a letter in the mail stating that I was accepted to summer school in the United States.

I jumped for joy. I will tell you that story in one of the other meditations in this book.

Galatians 6:9

Let us not become weary in doing good, for at the proper time we will reap a harvest if we do not give up. NIV

From Fear of Death to Abundant Life

I used to be afraid of many things. Especially of death.

I would become really self-aware. Hyper self-conscious. And then I would feel myself alive.

Then I would think: what if I died tomorrow? And a deep fear would grip me. I felt a deep vacuum, all the way to my bones.

Today I am here. Tomorrow no more. Today I am, tomorrow no longer.

So, I had to quickly think of something else, put some music on. Get distracted. Save the moment!

It was really discouraging. And it continued for a long time, and manifested itself in many ways, including fear of people, and fear of the future.

When Christ came to my heart, I felt really happy. I remember reading the Bible, and liking it.

And then one day I thought: what if I stop and allow myself to feel myself alive, and then dead like I used to do? Will the deep fear come back?

So, with a good measure of hesitation and nervousness I tried. And wow, I did not feel the fear. It was unbelievable.

I was at peace. Deep peace. The Prince of Peace had truly changed me.

Hebrews 2:14-15
Forasmuch then as the children are partakers of flesh and blood, he also himself likewise took part of the same; that through death he might destroy him that had the power of death, that is, the devil; And deliver them who through fear of death were all their lifetime subject to bondage. NIV

From Making Things Happen to Living in Grace

I was called "the excellent boy" when I was in Kindergarten. And believe me, it was not a great compliment. Now that I look back at it.

I felt pressure to perform. Yes, even at that young age. I don't know what it was. Maybe it was my fears of being less. Or my mother, who was always performance-oriented.

In any case, I remember throughout my life that I was expected to do more. Always more. When I completed my law degree, that same day, while walking away from the university, with the degree in my hand, my mother asked "when do you expect to complete your master's?"

When I was finishing my studies in the English language, I was asked: "how much time before you complete your French studies?"

At work, one of my bosses called me "barracuda" because she said that once I bit I would not let go. Until the job assigned to me was done. Another one of my bosses would say "don't tell him that it is impossible. He'll get it done."

And I got it done. I made things happen. Yes, I performed. But it was painful. I was so stressed out. I could not relax. I was self-conscious all the time. Even in the evenings. Even during downtime. I was always on.

Then grace came to me. The grace of God. Jesus whispering to my heart that I don't have to make things happen. In fact, I was not making things happen anyway. I thought I was making things happen. But it is always God who is in control of outcomes. Not me. Not you. So, I was deceived thinking that it was me.

It was God. And it needs to be God. It is too hard to try to do things on my own. I don't do that anymore. I pray. I ask Jesus for His help. I inquire about what the mind of Christ is on the matter. And I open my hands, and leave the outcome to Him. Life is not up to me anymore.

And before you get any ideas, no, I have not become a sluggard. Or mediocre. Or passive. Or inactive. Or laissez faire. That is not the proper response.

But, I have become more self-caring, and more compassionate with myself. And with others. I don't have a lot of negative self-talk anymore. I don't keep demanding things of myself. And putting myself down for apparent failures. And I don't worry about the outcome anymore. I am just diligent and faithful. And He provides the fruit.

Philippians 1:6
Being confident of this, that he who began a good work in you will carry it on to completion until the day of Christ Jesus. NIV

From Lack of Self-Management to Managing Complex Operations

I did not know how to govern myself when I was young. I would drink, too much. Sometimes I got drunk. I ate too much, until I had a tummy ache. I worked, too much. I partied, too much.

I was insistent, to the point of annoying. I would ask impertinent questions, and people would not want to get close to me.

We must have been 13 or so when we started drinking. My friend's parents had a small winery. And he would surreptitiously get a jar (yes, a jar!) of strong wine, and then we would drink it all. Sometimes by the glass. Bottoms up.

It was fun for a while, we would forget our pain, our anguish. And then of course the headache, the stomach ache. The promises to myself, not to do it again. Until the next weekend, when we would do it all over again.

Jesus changed it all. I gave my life to Him when I was doing my graduate studies. And then went on to the professional world. First as a clerk, then advisor, then manager, leader, and the like.

And one day I found myself managing complex operations. A staff of close to 3,000 people and a billion-dollar budget. It was exciting, challenging, taxing, and sometimes exhausting. But I learned, I delivered, I performed.

I did it for a while. I could feel the stress all over my chest. Vacations interrupted by office phone calls, review of e-mails, decisions to make. Less time for family, for my kids.

Not anymore. I am out of that race. It was a good race. But sometimes it felt like the rat race. Where no one wins. But, someone had to do it.

I am content not to manage complex operations anymore.

And I have learned to manage myself. To govern myself. Not by myself, because I can do nothing by myself. But by the power of Jesus in me.

Galatians 2:20

I have been crucified with Christ and I no longer live, but Christ lives in me. The life I now live in the body, I live by faith in the Son of God, who loved me and gave himself for me. NIV

From Emotionally Deprived to Crying Like a Baby

There I was. In San Antonio, Texas. 3 in the morning. My eye-shades on. My ear-plugs on. Curled up in bed -- fetal position. Crying my eyes out, because it was time to cry. It was a deep and heartfelt cry, a visceral cry that was overdue by more than 40 years.

I had been watching a video on the restoration of the heart, during a week of work with my office, in my hotel room. The topic was the pains of our childhood and how those affect our present life. We were encouraged to recall one such instance.

So, I remembered when I was about 11 years old. Alone. In a small town called Villazon, on the border between Bolivia and Argentina. Dirt streets, cold, full of strangers.

I had gone there with my mother, who was at the time in the business of buying merchandise from Argentina and selling it in Bolivia's capital, La Paz.

Our residence at the time was in Tupiza, another small town 100 kilometers away, much prettier, a warm valley with two beautiful rivers and red mountains. My birth place.

But I hated Villazon. Every time I got up at 4 am to get ready with my mother to take the 3-hour bus ride, on the dirt road from Tupiza to Villazon, I knew it was going to be unpleasant, to say the least.

My memories of that whole period are fuzzy, I don't know if it is that I cannot remember or I don't want to remember. And no, I tell you from the outset, nothing tragic happened, or really bad.

It was just the loneliness. The sense of abandonment and neglect. The sense that I had no one by my side.

All I remember is that my mother had to go someplace else to do business. I believe it was for a week. Maybe two, but it sure felt like an eternity. So, there I was, in a small and

Spartan room at a little cheap place called the Panamerican Hotel. Just a bed, and a small bed-table.

And I felt alone. And I cried. And cried. Until Jesus healed me. And restored me.

Matthew 11:28-30
Come to me, all you who are weary and burdened, and I will give you rest. Take my yoke upon you and learn from me, for I am gentle and humble in heart, and you will find rest for your souls. For my yoke is easy and my burden is light. NIV

From Loneliness to Companionship

My father had already left us, when I was 5 or so, and he had not come back to see us for at least 10 years, busy with his new family, his work, and his duties with the Lions Club.

My young sister stayed in La Paz, at a Catholic school. My brother farmed out to live with family or friends. So, there I was, in a small and Spartan room at a little cheap place called the Panamerican Hotel. Just a bed, and a small bed-table.

I don't think there was anything else in the room. No paintings, no decorations, nothing worth remembering. That town and everything about it was always cold, gloomy and cloudy, and it always felt foreign to me.

I remember that I attended school for a while in that town. One of the 14 or so different schools that I attended while completing primary and secondary school in at least 3 or 4 different cities in Bolivia. So I would not be able to name the school at all. Putting up with the bullying, the sea of strange faces passing in front and behind me in the school yard, I did not know anyone.

To top it off, I had my hard-shell briefcase (this style was called James Bond at the time), leather-like ivory texture, with my school books and papers. I guess I thought I would be James Bond, toughen up, put up with the world, and its onslaught on me. Most of the other students in that public school would not be able to afford a nice briefcase like that, so I stood out like a sore thumb, and that caused irritation and jealousy in them. They would call me snake-oil salesman and other things.

After a while I did not even mind. I was numb, I did not care. And I sure would not show any sign of weakness or vulnerability. Cry? No way, not even in private. Suck it up, deny, swallow hard, don't tell anyone, don't complain. Life is tough, get used to it.

When I was hungry I would just eat bread and some juice. For lunch or dinner, I remember going sometimes to a "restaurant" or so it was called. A tent-like place, I think the floor was dirt, covered with a corrugated metal roof. I had to bend to get in; I was taller than most people in that town. They served some kind of meat soup, with a round piece of bread.

What saved the day, to some extent, was the movie theater. That week without my mother or anyone else (or two weeks or three, I just don't recall) the feature presentation was Jesus of Nazareth. That was the only movie shown. So I watched it about 7 times, or more. It was about Jesus, when He was a child.

And He looked alone too, for some reason. I have this image of him in the movie, walking around on the dirt streets of his small town, eating bread, looking kind of dirty, and to me he was alone. Maybe he wasn't. But to me he was alone.

But I believe he was looking at me, yes, from the screen, in the cold and dark movie theater, with just a few people sitting here and there. He was alone, and I was alone. But he was looking at me.

Deuteronomy 31:8
The Lord himself goes before you and will be with you; he will never leave you nor forsake you. Do not be afraid; do not be discouraged. NIV

From Not Knowing Jesus to Being Known by Him

The only human contact I had during that week, from what I remember, was a guy that somehow became not my friend, but an acquaintance. We may have met at school. He was a little taller than me, and bigger, kind of clumsy. I guess he was alone too.

He came to my hotel room a couple of times, and we would take the little alcohol appliance where I boiled water for tea, and put it on, in the middle of the room. Then each one of us would take a little plastic bottle, with pharmacy alcohol in it, and squirt it through the appliance and into the wall.

Then our eyes would light up, as a line of fire would show up on the wall. Which would extinguish itself quickly, thankfully. And then another shot across the fire, boom, another line of fire on the other side of the room.

And sometimes we would get our hands wet with alcohol, and they would catch fire. Which, again, would extinguish itself quickly, thank God.

So there it is. That is my story for that time. You see, it is not that bad. Nothing too tragic.

Yet, I realized lying down in bed, that day at the hotel in San Antonio, that it was that story, those experiences that had been hurting me a lot. Maybe not so much that week by itself. But what it represented. The tip of the iceberg, of a life I lived in my childhood full of abandonment and neglect.

My poor mother tried her best, I cannot blame her, she did not know better. Her mother died when she was 5 and she never really had a father who loved her. Same with my father, he was also abandoned and neglected.

But that experience was symptomatic of that whole period of my life. And don't get me wrong. I also had good experiences and good friends then, especially back at my little warm town of Tupiza.

I had suppressed for so long the memories, the feelings, and woundings of my childhood, that I decided not to do that anymore. So I cried, and cried, and cried, in my hotel room. This time in a much better hotel, warm and cozy. And I did not feel alone.

Jesus was right there with me, healing me of all those wounds. And He actually showed me that He was there with me too, when I was 11 years old, and not just in the movie, but in reality. I just did not know Him then, but He knew me. And He loved me. And He loves me.

Jeremiah 1:5
Before I formed you in the womb I knew you, before you were born I set you apart; I appointed you as a prophet to the nations. NIV

From Either Or to Both and All

Notions of effort without fun, work without rest, life without choices, and a guilt complex for feeling good or having a good laugh are prevalent among some Christians. But, these notions may belong more to Ascetism than to Christianity.

Because we reflect God's image, we should also reflect His characteristics. And his characteristics include love, liberty, creativity, and yes, His sense of humor.

In addition, those who believe that they do not have the "right to have fun," in reality end up having fun anyway, but of course plagued by a strong sense of guilt. It happened to me too, believe me.

Don't you think it is time to liberate ourselves from this mental, spiritual, moral, and even physical slavery? It is time that we accept the fact that the only thing that Christ requires us to abandon from our past is sin.

The arts, science, politics, business, dance, music, economics, and other aspects of life are legitimate and open for Christian participation.

Rest is not only necessary, but indispensable and even ordained by God. Even God rested on the seventh day of His creation. Yes, praise God for the Sabbath.

Good movies, theater, folk or classical dance, social meetings, good food, sports, world travel, learning languages, and in general enjoying what God has made available to us is totally legitimate to all persons and especially to Christians as heirs of God's creation.

It is not necessary to choose between this world and the next. The Bible says that eternal life is to know God and His Son Jesus Christ (John 17:3).

If we know Jesus Christ now, and live in Him and He in us, our eternal life has already begun here on earth.

Let us live in a way that glorifies God in everything that we do!

Colossians 3:23-24

Whatever you do, work at it with all your heart, as working for the Lord, not for human masters, since you know that you will receive an inheritance from the Lord as a reward. It is the Lord Christ you are serving. NIV

From Abstinence to Self-Control

Many are given to abstinence. Though not seeing money as evil (as some other religions do), some Christians circulate the idea that since money may corrupt the person and since Jesus was apparently economically "poor" (and sided with the poor, they say) it is better not to go after money or establish a business, a corporation, etc.

It is better to just have enough to get by, so that we do not become "greedy." "Put your treasure in heaven" is the mantra.

On the question of alcohol, they have concluded that Jesus and His contemporaries were drinking grape juice, even at weddings. Thus, since wine or beer can lead us into sin, it is better to abstain altogether. And believe me, when I was young I had an issue with alcohol. Jesus took it away, and now I can enjoy a glass of wine, without feeling tempted or sinning.

Others, going further, and in order not to be "distracted" from the "work of the Lord," have decided to abstain from wives/husbands and/or children.

Still others, because science may prove that the Bible is wrong (so they reason) do not want to become scientists. Dance, contemporary music, the arts in general are seen as too "tempting," even "erotic" and thus not worthy of our attention.

They don't watch movies because "they contain some improper words" or "improper scenes." They instead demand Hollywood to produce "wholesome" and even "Christian" movies. However, why would they expect Hollywood (which presently has a different worldview and set of values) to produce the kind of movies Christians want?

What about Christians becoming good film-makers and producing wholesome movies? And some in fact have now done that very thing.

Plus, many of the Hollywood movies are in fact worth watching (you just have to ignore some bad language and scenes). If we had to totally avoid movies because of their issues, then we may as well quit work because our colleagues may use bad language, or behave inappropriately, or they may have issues.

A better principle than abstinence, one that the Bible does encourage us to adopt, is self-control. The fruits of the Spirit do not include abstinence (except of course abstinence from sin), but they do include self-control (Gal. 5:23, NAS).

We have the Holy Spirit inhabiting us. We are a new creation. And thus, we can enjoy God's creation. All of it. And it is your choice, of course. If you want to abstain, or you need to abstain, do so. But not everyone needs to do that, nor should we.

Acts 10:9-15

About noon the following day as they were on their journey and approaching the city, Peter went up on the roof to pray.

He became hungry and wanted something to eat, and while the meal was being prepared, he fell into a trance. He saw heaven opened and something like a large sheet being let down to earth by its four corners. It contained all kinds of four-footed animals, as well as reptiles and birds. Then a voice told him, "Get up, Peter. Kill and eat." "Surely not, Lord!" Peter replied. "I have never eaten anything impure or unclean." The voice spoke to him a second time, "Do not call anything impure that God has made clean." NIV

From Five-Fold to Infinite-Fold

I remember many years ago, shortly after my conversion, asking my pastor in Boston "how can I serve the Lord?" He told me, "in order to serve the Lord you need to be an evangelist, pastor, prophet, apostle or teacher in the church."

As I analyzed these options, and since none of them included a lawyer, I decided to set aside my law degree, my master's in law and economics, my specialization in negotiation from Harvard, and my career in general, because I really wanted to serve the Lord.

I went back to the pastor and excitedly told him I had decided to become an evangelist. He replied that that was great, but because the church didn't have funds to bring me on staff as a "full-time evangelist" that I should find some other kind of work to do in the meantime.

I ended up taking temporary work through a "temp" agency, waiting for an opening at the church. So, there I was, week after week, filing in alphabetical order bunches of disorganized papers that my boss had given me -- my temp work. Still waiting for an opening at the church.

There were two ladies there, also filing disorganized bunches of paper. One of them asked me: Have you ever studied anything? I told them about my degrees and the like. They could not believe it. After their shock, one of them confessed: We are working here because we never finished primary school.

Something hit me, hard, at that point. I felt out of place. As I reflected on my calling in life, I felt very strongly in my heart that the Lord was telling me "you are a lawyer." A couple of weeks later I felt that same prompting, "'You are a lawyer."

Something went off in my mind, and I understood that though many people leave aside careers, fortune, etc. to become evangelists and the like, that was not for me at that particular time. In fact, I felt the Lord Jesus telling me in my heart: I have called you to serve me, as a lawyer. I also learned at the time that Jesus Christ is our Advocate (our lawyer) before the Father.

And for decades since that is how I served Him, full-time.

Situations like this arise in part because church leaders, while rightly concentrating on the Gospel message, have caused an imbalance which has minimized the social impact that the church and Christians could have. The imbalance occurs because church leaders take the task of evangelizing the world not only as their own 9-to-5 or full-time call, but as everybody's call.

However, everybody has a call in terms of an occupation or vocation, but it is not necessarily street or other kinds of evangelism (the narrow sense of evangelism). We are also evangelizing in the broader sense of the word as we give testimony to Jesus Christ with our lives, the quality of our work, and as we please Him in everything that we do, no matter where we work.

And, of course, if we have a chance to share about Jesus explicitly we should do that as well.

1 John 2

My dear children, I write this to you so that you will not sin. But if anybody does sin, we have an advocate with the Father—Jesus Christ, the Righteous One. He is the atoning sacrifice for our sins, and not only for ours but also for the sins of the whole world.   NIV

From Potted to Planted

The Apostle Paul wrote that we are heavenly citizens (Philippians 3:20). But he was also fully aware of his Roman citizenship as evidenced in Acts 16:37 and other passages in the New Testament. In fact, three chapters of the book of Acts contain Paul's legal appeals based on his rights as a Roman citizen.

If the Lord chose to have three whole chapters in the Bible on this topic, then it must be because it is not a small matter. I also take my earthly, as well as my heavenly, citizenship seriously. And, that is why, having come to America as an immigrant, I then became an American.

Why would I "renounce and abjure all allegiance" -- as the Oath of Allegiance to the United States requires -- to my country of origin, thus creating a permanent division between myself and family, friends, and the land of my birth, to become an American?

Moreover, why not just reason, as some Christians do, "I am a citizen of the Kingdom of God, therefore it does not matter what nationality I have, or if I have two or more."

The reason why is that America deserves better from her immigrants, and also from her native-born. It is the only way that we will be really productive in our society.

A whole-hearted commitment to America is also good for immigrants themselves. The psychological toll of people who have lived in America for 15 or 20 years and still have one foot here and one in "their country" is tremendous.

Let us make this our home. Let us make this country our own. Let us unpack, not just our luggage, but also our minds. Let us seek not just rights, but also responsibilities.

Ultimately, like those who came before us, let us pledge "our Lives, our Fortunes, and our sacred Honor" for the betterment of the United States of America. As we do that, we are also helping the rest of the world.

Acts 16:37

But Paul said to the officers: "They beat us publicly without a trial, even though we are Roman citizens, and threw us into prison. And now do they want to get rid of us quietly? No! Let them come themselves and escort us out." NIV

From Loud Dislike to Quiet Admiration

I am an immigrant, a newcomer. When I arrived in America many years ago, I realized that an amazing gap existed between the material abundance and great freedom in the United States compared to the country that I left.

English, having become the language of international communication, is studied and spoken the world over. One time, during negotiations at the United Nations, we were all speaking through translators and earphones, because you have to respect every country's identity, but when weeks went by and we were getting really tired, everyone took their earphones off, and we came to an agreement, in English.

Though many people do not acknowledge it openly, there is a sense of admiration worldwide for the United States and its accomplishments.

The world is proud of America -- though, again, many people would not say it aloud. People around the world feel that

America embodies what they would want to achieve in terms of political freedom, economic prosperity, cultural diversity and richness.

Moreover, since the United States as a modern nation was started basically from scratch and has absorbed and benefited from millions of immigrants from all corners of the world, people in other countries feel that they have had a major contribution in the making of our wonderful America.

America was engineered from the beginning. Her Constitution was drafted and discussed word by word. The American government was established with clear responsibilities and limitations based on the notion of a society based on unalienable rights that come from God.

Jeremiah 29:11
"For I know the plans I have for you," declares the Lord, "plans to prosper you and not to harm you, plans to give you hope and a future." NIV

From a Minority Complex to Leading the Majority

I hope you realize that the idea of "minority" is more than anything else a state of mind. Though in the past there was open discrimination and abuse and coerced segregation against ethnic groups, smaller religious organizations, and others, there is now no legal or compelling reason to continue to be segregated.

While many Christian churches and individuals are substantially involved with the community and having a positive impact, too many other Christians have adopted the minority mentality.

The term "minority" keeps surfacing as Christians adopt it for themselves, especially as they struggle for access to the public square. However, unlike many countries around the world, in modern America you can choose to belong to a minority, but you don't have to.

The minority mentality expresses itself among Christians as

follows: First, Christians have developed a sense of "distinctiveness," believing that we are too different to be equal or to even mingle with the rest of society.

Others, on the other extreme, have just "blended in" with society and abandoned any sense of distinctiveness. Second, many Christians do not trust elected and non-elected officials that do not belong to the Christian community. There is an automatic rejection of people that do not identify themselves openly as Christian, thus fueling the idea of categorical representation or group identity.

This idea proposes that a particular group can only be understood, empathized with and represented by members of that group. This creates a situation where individuals will only trust members of their "own people."

Paradoxically, many Christians do not want to be political leaders themselves. When they talk about political leadership in the Bible, their favorite examples are Nehemiah, who was an aid to King Artaxerxes and Joseph, who was second to Pharaoh.

It is as if we consider ourselves only good enough to be second to the political leader -- especially to advise him or her on spiritual matters -- but not really the leader himself/herself. Why not talk about David, who was the king and leader of all his people?

2 Samuel 5:4-5
David was thirty years old when he became king, and he reigned forty years. In Hebron he reigned over Judah seven years and six months, and in Jerusalem he reigned over all Israel and Judah thirty-three years.

From Loving Just Hymns to Loving Clean Floors

Concerning the "call," we know that God does not have first and second class calls. God is no respecter of persons.

The concept of the universal priesthood of all believers goes directly against the establishment of ecclesiastical hierarchies or dominant classes in the Kingdom of God. In the church there should be leaders, not lords.

The word "minister" means deacon or servant. Romans 13 refers to government authorities as "ministers of God," and not only that but as "servants," hence the Prime Minister of the country is the prime servant. Government authorities "give their full time to governing" (Ro. 13:6, NIV), that is, they are full-time ministers of God.

Romans 13 also suggests that even non-Christians could be ministers for God's purposes. Thus, if political and military authorities can be ministers of God, why not an economist, a homemaker, a carpenter, or any other Christian that is performing their profession or occupation in obedience to God?

A Christian can have a call in his or her life to be a professor, evangelist, electrician, mother, or may dedicate himself or herself to any other activity as long as they are obeying God.

Likewise, being a pastor or an evangelist does not automatically place anyone within the will of God (see Matt, 7:21-23). All Christians should evangelize (in the strict sense of sharing the gospel) when the opportunity arises.

Yet, one should not overlook the fact that we are also evangelizing (in the wider sense of the word) and discipling the nations when we perform our daily activities with excellence.

As Martin Luther said, "The maid who sweeps the kitchen is doing God's will just as much as the monk who prays -- not because she may sing a Christian hymn while she sweeps, but because God loves clean floors." And he added, "The

Christian shoemaker does his Christian duty not by placing little crosses on the shoes, but by making good shoes because God is interested in good craftsmanship."

Thus, the ministry of the Christian is exercised twenty-four hours a day, 365 days a year. We are ministers when we pray, sleep, study, eat, work, take a vacation, read the Bible or read the newspaper.

Everything we do should be done unto the Lord (or we better not do it), and therefore our profession or occupation, or any other activity has value and is pleasing to God even if we are not "evangelizing" (in the strict sense of the word) or doing any other inherently "religious" activity.

Romans 13:1-2
Let everyone be subject to the governing authorities, for there is no authority except that which God has established. The authorities that exist have been established by God. Consequently, whoever rebels against the authority is

rebelling against what God has instituted, and those who do so will bring judgment on themselves. NIV

From Overemphasis to Delicate Balance

Our nation, demands our attention, energy, and resources. Whether it is voting or running for the local school board or other public offices, paying taxes, or complying with all sorts of regulations and laws established by the government, we feel pulled and sometimes even consumed, by our responsibilities to the state.

And let us remember to rest (I am preaching to obsessive-compulsives like myself). There are twice as many references to rest in the Bible than there are for work.

Concerning physical exercise, which is part of our leisure/self-renewal, the Apostle Paul did say that "bodily exercise profiteth little" (1 Tim. 4:8, KJV). Thus, some reason, we need not bother with it (the ones on the other extreme simply want to "burn out for Jesus").

We must remember, however, that Paul, as most of his contemporaries, walked to most places he went (no wonder he did not need jogging).

Therefore, he did not stress the importance of physical exercise (in that verse he was emphasizing spiritual godliness), though what we may understand, as rendered in other Bible translations, is that physical exercise is of some, albeit limited, value.

Additionally, Paul frequently made references to athletes as models for spiritual disciplines. Our bodies, says the Bible, are the temple of the Holy Spirit. Some of us, though, due to an overweight condition, look more like the cathedrals of the Holy Spirit.

I am not talking about all of us becoming supermodels or body-builders, I am talking about not overlooking the sin of gluttony and our carelessness with our physical condition which can seriously impair our productivity and mission.

Finally, many of us Christians, in addition to having to deal with family, work, church, and nation have to take care of academic pursuits. No wonder life can become such a zoo!

So how do we maintain our sanity, be responsible and faithful as we juggle our limited time, resources, and energy among these important and often-times competing spheres of life? And more importantly, how can we be excellent with our family, work, church, nation, and studies all at the same time?

One of the ways to do this is by allocating time, energy, and resources to each one of these areas so as to allow them to coexist in a delicate balance.

Romans 12:1-2
Therefore, I urge you, brothers and sisters, in view of God's mercy, to offer your bodies as a living sacrifice, holy and pleasing to God—this is your true and proper worship. Do not conform to the pattern of this world, but be transformed by the renewing of your mind. Then you will be able to test

and approve what God's will is—his good, pleasing and perfect will. NIV

From Black and White to Multicolor Existence

The Bible tells us that Jesus Christ came to give us life -- not life in the sense of simple biological survival or as opposed to being dead. He came to give us abundant life. Life in abundance implies primarily to know God, to have surrendered to His Son Jesus Christ and to have the Holy Spirit living inside of us.

While this is essential and fundamental for a true abundant life, there is still more. The immensity and greatness of the Creation of God does not exist without a purpose. Nothing of what God has created is unnecessary or insignificant or He would not have created it.

On the contrary, everything in the Creation of God has an order, a meaning, and a purpose. Minerals feed the plants, plants in turn feed the animals, and the animals feed the people. The sun, moon, and stars provide light, warmth, and determine the climatological conditions and seasons for life to reproduce itself on our planet.

Rain, wind, and air are indispensable elements to preserve life. In summary, each component of the Creation is essential to abundant life as a whole and to make life worth living.

Men and women, as the summit of God's creation, are the most important and direct beneficiaries of what nature has to offer. Some think that consuming "the minimum biologically indispensable" to survive and continue to work suffices. Why bother with well prepared and delicious dishes or choosing from a variety of culinary alternatives?

However, we must ask ourselves, why would have God created hundreds of colors, flavors, and fragrances? Why such a wide variety of fruits? What would be the meaning of natural landscapes and beautiful views? Why would we have the possibility to create an infinite mixture of musical rhythms?

Finally, why would such a variety in every area of life -- human, animal, vegetal, mineral -- exist?

If God had wanted us to live on bread and water and have a black and white existence, He could have created a simple and unidimensional world, one that only has the minimal indispensable, and without the possibility of choice and variety.

However, the fact is that the Creator made the world multi-dimensional and richly diverse, thus giving us a wonderful habitat as well as providing further insight into His own nature. Who can doubt that God has infinite imagination, joviality, and even a sense of humor?

Yes, just look around at the elephants and giraffes (or our own faces) to see evidence of this, and be amazed.

Psalm 19:1
The heavens declare the glory of God; the skies proclaim the work of his hands. NIV

From Guilty Feeling to Pure Fun

Sometimes we may wonder about what the concepts of entertainment and fun may mean for the Christian. For example, have you ever been having fun and laughing hard, only to suddenly be overcome with fear and a sense that something sad, and painful may come your way later?

"I'm laughing too much, I hope nothing bad happens to me afterwards," seems to be the thought that assaults our minds and makes us feel guilty.

We also notice in some Christian circles a strong ascetic, almost monastic message -- "we must abandon the things of this world," "we shouldn't get distracted with things on this earth," "dedicate yourself only to the things of God," "I do not have fun, I only work for the Lord," and "there is no time for fun, the Lord is coming soon, we must evangelize."

Let us analyze the meaning of the word "world." Biblically, at least two renderings exist. One, the most common and the most utilized, refers to "world" in the sense of sin, evil, self-sufficiency and rejection of God. In summary, "world" is everything that is contrary to God.

Thus, we read "therefore, whoever wishes to be a friend of the world makes himself an enemy of God" (James 4:4).

A second, less prevalent and less well-understood rendering of "world" simply refers to the people of this planet, the planet itself, and the universe or Creation. Thus, we read John 3:16 "for God so loved the world that He gave His only begotten Son, that whoever believes in Him should not perish, but have eternal life."

Of course, we know that God does not love sin. Therefore, when the Scriptures state that God loves the world, we understand that God loves the people of His creation and creation itself.

Extreme pietism encourages Christians to live a passive life, praying and studying the Bible, enclosed exclusively within the four walls of the church, and at the expense of all other societal activities (arts, culture, politics, business, economics, law, entertainment, etc.).

The logical consequence is the abandonment of the world, the rejection of society in general, and the despising of that which is not overtly "religious" or "spiritual." This, of course, is a misinterpretation of the Bible, of history, and of life in general. Unless you have been truly called by God to be a monk or a hermit. Most have not.

Let us live life, in all its dimensions, to the fullest. That is what Jesus came to give us.

John 10:10
The thief comes only to steal and kill and destroy; I have come that they may have life, and have it to the full. NIV

From Emotionally Deprived to Passionate Lover

Growing up, I don't remember having strong emotions.

I thought it was improper to shout at sports arenas. I felt embarrassed when people got loud and cheerful.

My feeling was that I needed to be in control. Of my mind and my emotions. I could not just jump and yell. How juvenile! How crass for people to do so!

Once I became a Christian, I went to church and people were saying "amen!" really loud. I thought: "how disrespectful."

Then I read in the Bible that Jesus had strong emotions. He would yell. He would weep. He became hot with anger. He would be kind to the children. He would love with a passion.

And I wanted that. I was so tired of being flat-lined. Cool. Cold blooded. All the time. I wanted to feel.

So I prayed. I asked God to release my emotions. To let me experience things. To have strong feelings.

And the tears started flowing. I could empathize with others. Even cry at the movies. Or get really excited about a good football or soccer game. And cheer! And yes, love, deeply, like I've never loved before.

I had to ask God to tone it down a bit. I was crying about everything. Getting moved by everything going on around me. Now when I go to the mall around Christmas, I am overwhelmed by the lights, the music, the decorations!

But, it feels good. I feel good.

Mark 10:21
Then Jesus beholding him loved him. KJV

From Feeling Shame to Extending Empathy

I remember a time during middle school. There was a boy who would annoy me constantly. It was getting to be too much. So, one day I saw him at the Principal's office, with two other people. And I thought, they must be getting on his case, because he is a troublemaker. So, on the spur of the moment, I told them that he was bothering me too.

Yikes, it did not go well. Instead of finding allies against him, they all turned against me. Turns out that the two others were his parents, and they all sided with him and against me!

I felt shame. I felt alone. And I regretted that I opened my mouth.

You know, that warm feeling that creeps into your cheeks. That makes you want to disappear immediately and never show up again.

Many such instances accompanied me during my life.

But not anymore. I have learned from Jesus. He was on the cross, absolutely tortured and disfigured by those around Him. And the only thing He said was: Father, forgive them for they don't know what they are doing.

It is not just about me anymore. Me taking offense at what people say. Or thinking poor me, and taking it personally. Or even worse, lashing out, fighting back, paying in kind. Eye for an eye.

It is about them. When something like that happens now, like someone yelling, or reacting in anger, or saying something inappropriate, I take a deep breath (inhale deeply, hold, exhale, and hold, repeat, it helps a lot!).

And then I think about the other person. Is he in pain? Is she stressed out? Could I have acted or spoken more gracefully in order to help with the situation? What could be making them react this way?

Empathy starts growing inside of me. I immediately start feeling compassion toward others. And I can even pray for that other person. And trust the Lord with the situation.

Ephesians 4:32
Be kind and compassionate to one another, forgiving each other, just as in Christ God forgave you. NIV

From Old School to the Fletcher School

I graduated with a Law Degree from the University of San Andres, in La Paz, Bolivia. That University was founded in 1830.

A little over a hundred years later, in 1933, The Fletcher School of Law and Diplomacy, at Tufts University was founded in Boston. From which I graduated with a Master's in Law.

There were only 2 years between obtaining my law degree, and my master's. But what a difference it made. It felt like a hundred years.

A miracle was needed. I did not have money, my work credentials were thin, and my English was incipient.

But, thanks be to God, I applied -- asking Fletcher to waive the application fee since I was making only $50 a month at my cashier job in Bolivia.

Weeks later, I got a shiny envelope in the mail, with beautiful high relief letters, from Fletcher. It said that I was not accepted to the regular program. But I was welcome to come to the Summer School.

I ran, I was so excited. Finished all my paperwork at my law school, and defended my thesis.

Within days I got a ticket, and took a taxi, resigning from my cashier job on the way to the airport.

Once at Fletcher, I got one of the best grades in class and was accepted to the regular program. I was one of only 2 students out of close to 100 on the waiting list who were accepted.

One of many miracles in my life.

Zechariah 4:10
Do not despise these small beginnings, for the Lord rejoices to see the work begin. NLT

From Loner to Team Player

I grew up thinking that something was wrong with me. Some of the people that knew me said that I belonged with the anti-socials.

The anti-socials were a group of 4 or so guys, and I was one of them. We did not belong with the regular groups, the clicks, the mainstream so to speak. And we were proud of it. Go it alone. Kind of, because we were not really alone. We had each other.

My favorite sports were individual sports, not team sports. I liked swimming, biking, and racquetball. You on that side. Me on this other side. Don't touch me. Much less break my nose.

Not only did I not like groups of guys playing together and being physical with each other, but I was afraid of breaking my bones. Some of the guys I knew would have whole armors made up of their leg cast, shoulder cast, and so on. I never broke a bone. And, knock on wood, I want to keep it that way.

I realized more recently that it was not just the fear of breaking a bone, or my dislike for big groups. The big reason was that I did not know how to negotiate. How to give and take. How to be pals, peers, equals, and work it out. Even through conflict.

Instead, I gave myself 2 choices: I was in charge. Or someone else was in charge, and I followed. Of course, my strong inclination was to be in charge.

Jesus Christ changed all that. I understood that I am a co-heir, that I belong to a community of people, that I am no better or worse than anyone else. We are all on the same boat, and we need to work together.

I like communion now, I actually crave it. I don't have to be the boss anymore. And I don't have to feel that others need to control me. I am a team player, a good sport, and I feel all the more mature and balanced because of it.

So, whenever I am tempted to go it alone again, I remember that the Holy Spirit inhabits me, that I live in Him, that my wife and I are partners as well as lovers, and that I get to live life with my fellow human beings. As brothers and sisters.

As someone once said, the quality of your life is the quality of your relationships.

Hebrews 13:1
Keep on loving one another as brothers and sisters. NIV

From Pankration to Jiu Jitsu

Pankration was a sport in ancient Greece that combined boxing and wrestling. With this approach you face your opponent full force, take their blows, impart some blows on them, and utilize a lot of force against each other. A lot of brute force, to be more specific.

That was my modus operandi, my particular way of doing things, in the past. If someone opposed me, I would try to fight back frontally. Not necessarily in physical form, since I never really fought physically with anyone (my father had left, so no one was there to teach me how to do it, and thankfully I did not have need for it, my friends did the work for me!).

If someone sent me a tough e-mail, I would respond immediately, in kind. Someone said something harsh to my face, I would look at them and give them a few choice words of my own. If someone had their high-beam headlights on in the car, I would quickly switch mine on. Give them of their own medicine, as a friend of mine liked to say.

Well, that only works for a while. And it wears you out. Too much energy spent. For too little a result.

Later on I took some martial arts classes, particularly Tae Kwon Do. In martial arts you learn a different approach. Instead of confronting the opponent head on, you get out of the way. That is, you maximize the force exerted by the opponent against the opponent.

For example, if someone tries to punch you, instead of punching back, you take their hand, continue in the direction of their punch, open their hand in the process, twist it, and utilize the weight of the opponent's body to put pressure (that is the medical term for pain), on their arm.

Isn't it how Jesus handled difficult situations? When a king asked Him controversial questions, He stayed quiet. When His disciples asked Him to take control in His own hands, He went away to the mountain, to pray. When James and John asked Him to call down fire from Heaven to burn their opponents, Jesus rebuked them. And yes, in the end, though people were asking Him to destroy His opponents, He chose to die on the cross.

At first sight it looks like Jesus was defeated. That He was a loser. That the bad guys won. But what was the real story?

Well, we know that resurrection cannot come without death. That His Kingship over the whole Heaven and Earth could not come without being a servant. That the Truth would prevail over falsehood. That the last would be first.

Yes, lovers of Christ, our lives need to be counterintuitive, sometimes they don't make sense. Except as we see them through the lens of eternity.

Ephesians 6:12-13
For our struggle is not against flesh and blood, but against the rulers, against the authorities, against the powers of this

dark world and against the spiritual forces of evil in the heavenly realms. Therefore, put on the full armor of God, so that when the day of evil comes, you may be able to stand your ground, and after you have done everything, to stand.   NIV

From Losing her Degree to Finding Life

My mother was very smart, and well educated. But she had no gift for business. She tried hard -- selling things, hair salon, import-export, with little success.

Nothing seemed to work. It was more the loss of the investment than the profits. We survived, but we needed to thrive. Sometimes we had things to eat. Sometimes little.

My sister, my brother and I learned to make bread. We would take flour, make the bread, decorate it with pieces of banana, give it the shape of a dinosaur. And then eat bread, and coffee, for a couple of weeks, until my mother came back from her latest business trip, bringing a lot of food, which we would consume quickly.

It was tight, and tiring. My mother would worry, get depressed, sleep more than needed.

Then, one day, it had to be God because it was crazy, my mother decided to check the pictures and other stuff that was at the bottom of one of the closets.

She starts unrolling the big photographs that were held by an elastic band. She looks at them; we look at them.

Then she picks up another rolled up paper, and it turns out to be her degree. Yes, her law degree!

It was really crazy. It was a law degree that she had received at one of the best universities in the world at the time, the University of Buenos Aires.

She looks at us and asks: do you think I could do something with this? We look at each other, astonished, and the only thing we managed to say, with a big sigh of relief, was, yes!

So, off she went, armed with her powerful academic weapon under her arm, and got a lawyer's job with the local government. And life got much much better for all of us from then on.

Matthew 13:44-46

The kingdom of heaven is like treasure hidden in a field. When a man found it, he hid it again, and then in his joy went and sold all he had and bought that field. Again, the kingdom of heaven is like a merchant looking for fine pearls. When he found one of great value, he went away and sold everything he had and bought it. NIV

From Hopeless Observers to Active Change Agents

You may have been wondering why we as Christians are not more effective in changing our world for the better. In slowing down the decay in our society, in confronting the corruption in our government and other levels of society, in motivating our hopeless and errant youth, in stopping family disintegration, and generally being the salt and light that Christ commands us to be.

Could it be because of our attitudes and beliefs about our purpose here on earth, about the end times, about what is really important and spiritual, and about what really pleases the Lord?

One colleague in the office recently said that his office work is not Christian. It's just work. Others think that only going to church is Christian, or going on missions.

In fact, the whole idea about work and life balance gives credence to this erroneous idea that what we do during the day, 8 hours a day, for 5 days or more a week, for most of our lives, is not life, much less Christian.

Many Christians express deep doubts, dilemmas, frustration, and guilt. Others are desperate to find some kind of comfort, some kind of assurance that what we are doing most days is not a waste, is not useless, and in fact could even be pleasing to the Lord.

I have come to believe that at some point in our lives we can be students, then parents, then professionals, then grandparents, then missionaries, then students again. Or some of these simultaneously. It all matters to the Lord. It is all Christian. It all advances the Kingdom of God.

So, let's abandon double-mindedness. Let's have an integrated faith. Let's serve God every day, wherever we are, whatever we are doing.

Maybe then, we will all go forth and effectively "turn our world upside down."

1 Thessalonians 4:11-12

Make it your ambition to lead a quiet life: You should mind your own business and work with your hands, just as we told you, so that your daily life may win the respect of outsiders and so that you will not be dependent on anybody. NIV

From Non-Essential to Essential

The federal government shutdown, which takes place once every few years due to budget disagreements in Congress, had America wondering whether those close to 2 million federal employees were "non-essential."

What if it had been the millions of Christians (born again Christians) that had been "shut down" from America's public life? Would they too be considered "non-essential"? To illustrate this point, let us just imagine for a moment that God had decided to "shut down" all Christians, supernaturally and silently, out of the United States, tomorrow.

Most of the government would continue its normal operations, with some absentees. The media might broadcast their regular "prime-time" news unaware of what had just happened. By and large, at least in the short run, academia, science, the entertainment industry, and the arts would be mostly unaffected. It would be business as usual.

By Sunday, perhaps people would start noticing that many churches (not all) did not open. Clergy and substantial numbers of parishioners would be missing. However, while the absence of Christians would create a void in family circles, schools, and churches, it would certainly not bring the day-to-day operations of most sectors of public life to a screeching halt.

On the other hand, what would have happened if this sudden disappearance of Christians had taken place during America's founding era? Would this have affected the operations of government, education, science, business, and academia? Certainly the disappearance would have been detrimental to most segments of public life, and in some instances would have caused them to crumble. Society could not have but noticed the difference.

Why is Christian influence so lacking in today's society? The increasing secularization of society and its systematic exclusion of Christians and Christian ideas only partially account for the lack of Christian presence in public life.

Harvard University was founded in 1638 by Reverend John Harvard, just 18 years after the arrival of the Pilgrims in New England. Among its "Rules and Precepts," it was established that "Everyone shall consider the main end of his life and studies is, to know God and Jesus Christ which is eternal life."

Its first presidents reasoned that there could be no true knowledge or wisdom without Jesus Christ. Harvard's original coat-of-arms depicted three books and the word "Veritas" (Truth), together with the words "Christo et Ecclesiae" (for Christ and the Church). One of the books was closed signifying that only God can know everything. As time went on Christians at Harvard became luke-warm about their convictions. "Christo" and "Ecclesiae" were deleted from its motto.

The third book was opened, placing human beings on the same level as God. "Veritas" remained untouched, but this truth was without Christ. In so doing, Harvard opened its arms wide to embrace anti-Christian theories and perspectives. Knowledge was emphasized over truth, or as II Timothy 3:7 puts it: "always learning and never able to come to the knowledge of the truth."

Proverbs 4:7

The beginning of wisdom is this: Get wisdom. Though it cost all you have, get understanding. NIV

From Squatting to Bowing in Prayer

The torturous feeling of the "in-between mentality" -- people that do not want to be here, but are still here; people that would like to be in Heaven, but are not there yet -- reminds me of the "little-ease." Albert Camus, the French existentialist, describes this prison cell with "ingenious dimensions" in which "one was forgotten for life" called the little-ease:

"It was not high enough to stand up in nor yet wide enough to lie down in. One had to take on an awkward manner and live on the diagonal; sleep was a collapse, and waking a squatting. Mon cher, there was genius." (The Fall, p.109).

Our best days are not in the past, but ahead of us. Our present societal leadership that purports not to believe in a living God, that sees no mission or purpose on this earth, that considers humans a product of chance and no better (often worse) than the animals, and that believes that once we die, we become dust with no further life or transcendent purpose, cannot keep the prosperity and freedom that America still possesses.

Christians, on the other hand, are people endowed with a worldview that is complete and certain, which progresses from creation through redemption and moves to a final climax when Jesus Christ completes the establishment of His Kingdom on earth as it is in Heaven.

Christians are people who will never die. People who have access to God Himself, and have been given the assurance that God will be with them wherever they go. Shouldn't we Christians be able to lead, inspire and give a sense of direction and purpose not only to other Christians, but to all Americans?

Could it be possible that God has left us here on earth as a way to give us humans an opportunity to utilize and develop our skills, our emotions, our consciences, and thus improve our social interactions?

Could it be that the Lord wants us to exercise our God-given creativity, will, and mental capacities to explore the universe He has created? The Lord may be interested to see what we will do and how we will use the tremendous blessings and resources he has given us both at the personal and societal level.

James 4:10
Humble yourselves before the Lord, and He will lift you up.
NIV

From Pretending to Authenticity

The persistent message from the pulpit accentuates the importance of being "called" by God to the "full time ministry" -- that is, to be pastors, evangelists, teachers and the like.

However, the overwhelming majority of Christians are neither pastors nor evangelists or any of the other 5-fold ministry offices, and no one would think it reasonable for all of them to be so. Does this mean that they are outside the will of God, or missing out on something that God has for them?

Another idea is that if those not involved in "full-time ministry" such as homemakers, economists, or carpenters want to "redeem" their abilities, they should use their profession as a "means" for evangelism.

In other words, their studies, profession and occupation are only acceptable if they allow them to "preach the gospel" in their school, workplace, or neighborhood, or to enter those countries that are "closed" to missionaries.

From this perspective, being a good medical doctor, a dedicated father, or a skilled carpenter, simply would not be good enough to please God. Thus, pastors and preachers with good intentions, and a great zeal for God and evangelism, may be helping to breed a generation of frustrated, and mediocre students and professionals.

However, our performance in academics or in our profession does matter to the Lord. Colossians 3:23, 24 says that "Whatever you do, work at it with all your heart, as working for the Lord, not for men . . . It is the Lord Christ you are serving."

Many students and professionals have no other source but the church to affirm them in their particular vocation. Therefore, it is urgent that ecclesiastical leaders gain a more accurate understanding of this topic.

From the Bible, we can infer that any Christian that is performing legitimate activities -- whether it be economics, evangelism, homemaking, politics or business -- with honesty, dedication and integrity is acting in the service of God (1 Peter 4:10, 11).

1 John 3:18
Dear children, let us not love with words or speech but with actions and in truth. NIV

From Removing to Renewing Our Minds

The excesses of rationalism and its heavy reliance on the mind without regard to Scripture may be to blame for some Christians, particularly Charismatics, distrusting reason, intellectuals, doctrines, and ideologies.

However, sole reliance on emotions and feelings is no adequate response to this problem. This kind of emotionalism has even been compared to superstition, when used as a substitute for rationalism.

The insistence on faith-healing and becoming prosperous through prayer has led many Charismatics to believe that the "miraculous" is the rule and the "natural" is secondary.

Personal responsibility takes second place as character flaws and sins are blamed on demons from which one needs to be "delivered."

Some time ago, a Pentecostal leader was surprised when I

asked him why the curriculum for his new Ministerial Training Center did not include the subject of Church History. He simply said "We are training Christians to evangelize the people now, today. We do not need to study Church History."

Thus, rationalism has been abandoned together with the study of systematic theology and church history, placing even the Bible in a secondary role after "experiencing and being anointed by the Holy Spirit."

It is common to hear phrases such as "it does not matter if you know the Bible well, the important thing is to be filled by the Holy Spirit, and be led by Him." Indiscriminate acceptance of extra-biblical "revelations" and prophecies is also common.

The message of salvation of souls, along with the belief that Jesus Christ will return in a few years, months, or even days, or that the "rapture" will take place at any moment, has caused some of these churches to develop a very short-sighted perspective of life.

If time is short, they reason, we should all focus on evangelism and the salvation of souls.

Why bother participating in politics, or studying economics or engineering? Why dedicate ourselves to such "mundane" roles as law, psychology, or even worse philosophy?

Romans 12:2
Do not conform to the pattern of this world, but be transformed by the renewing of your mind. Then you will be able to test and approve what God's will is—his good, pleasing and perfect will. NIV

From Poor Example to Godly Testimony

The ongoing religious resurgence in many parts of the world, gives Christians an extraordinary opportunity to transform the world in all areas of life. Alternatively, this enormous spiritual energy could be spent in individual and religious self-gratification if it is not externalized properly toward society.

There are some major and interrelated areas of special concern which could seriously hinder Christians and especially Charismatics' (fastest growing) contribution to society.

First, the misconstrued division between religious and secular. Second, the apparent conflict between emotions and reason. And third, the emphasis on the "call to ministry" and the end of the world.

The pietistic notion that divides the religious from the secular and assigns more importance to the spirit realm over the material world has a long history. In today's church, this pietistic view has created, what I, a Christian/Charismatic myself, can only call a religious paranoia.

By this I mean that church members concentrate and place great importance solely on "religious" matters at the expense of every other activity or aspect of life. For instance, many believe they are doing "spiritual things" only when they are reading their Bible, attending church, or praying.

Everything else, such as studying, working, sleeping, eating, etc. is just "secular" or "worldly." "Spiritual" or "Christian" music is that which explicitly refers to the Bible or to Jesus.

Another example is the overemphasis on tithing. One pastor recently said "ten percent of his or her income is the least a church member can give to God." Thus, money spent on children's education, food, business, housing, or any other legitimate expense is not perceived as being given to God. Church takes precedence over family, work, and social life.

This pattern of thought which has caused an ecclesiastical atrophy, or a lack of growth and expansion beyond church activities, has resulted in Christians despising or at least minimizing their studies or professions and the value of their work.

They have also minimized other areas of societal life such as education, business, and politics, the latter largely seen as Satan's domain.

As a result, many Christians have become mediocre in their non-church-related activities and are giving a poor testimony to society at large. Why would anyone want to become like us?

1 Timothy 4:12
Don't let anyone look down on you because you are young, but set an example for the believers in speech, in conduct, in love, in faith and in purity. NIV

From Otherworldly to a Land of Milk and Honey

Some church leaders seem to think that the task of evangelizing the world is the primary function of the family, the state, our workplace, etc. Obviously, it is not, at least not in the narrow sense of evangelism. But, there is a magnet to this type of thinking, maybe because of the deeply emotional church services.

It is Sunday morning and somewhere a full-blown concert is underway with a 12-piece band, singing, shouting, whistling, clapping, and dancing. No, it is not a famous rock band elating the youth, but a typical Charismatic church service.

People are deeply immersed in the service, their eyes closed, some crying, others singing at the top of their voice or speaking in tongues, and still others lifting faces and hands toward heaven.

The music goes on and on in a crescendo, from soft strains to a fast, dynamic, arresting rhythm. The music leader encourages the congregation to express themselves, to get involved.

After a long time, and as people fully express their emotions, they reach the climatic point, as the music becomes deafening. Then it slows down and moves the congregation into a quiet time of meditation, prayer, and worship of God.

Now comes the pastor, who encourages the whole congregation to shout and clap, as loud as possible, as they praise God. The message is simple: the only way to salvation is Jesus Christ. You must convert now, while there is still time.

No more drunkenness, immorality, cheating, and lying. The Lord is coming soon and we must all prepare to go with Him. Once the congregation seems to be convicted enough, or at least impacted by the message, the music softly restarts while the pastor asks all who want to accept the Lord to come forward.

It is also time for supernatural healing. As the leaders pray, some people start falling down ("slain in the Spirit") which is seen as an outward expression of the Holy Spirit coming into their lives.

As people are prayed for and find the comfort they need, they start leaving in a quiet procession of radiant faces. They are convinced the Lord is coming back any time soon. They will make sure they bring their relatives and friends to next week's meeting, if the "Rapture" has not yet occurred.

Thus, the Charismatic attraction continues to attract new members, literally by the hundreds and even thousands. Much of it is good. The overemphasis on evangelism and Heaven is not.

Exodus 3:8
So I have come down to rescue them from the hand of the

Egyptians and to bring them up out of that land into a good and spacious land, a land flowing with milk and honey. NIV

From Ambivalent Christians to World Changers

Traveling throughout the United States and around the world, I have, time and again, encountered Christians who have told me, or expressed something to this effect:

A YOUNG LAW STUDENT: "I am so confused. I thought that working hard in Law school would please the Lord. However, other Christians told me that if I really want to please the Lord I should go to Seminary."

AN ECONOMIST: "I have been a Christian for 10 years, but I still don't know how my work relates to my faith."

A CIVIL SERVANT: "I cannot wait to get out of my office so I can go do something spiritual, like reading my Bible."

A MOTHER: "I am so bored with changing diapers, cooking, and cleaning the house. I wish I could have a ministry and do something for the Lord."

A TV PRODUCER: "I produce wholesome, family-oriented programs. But because I do not mention God or Jesus, or the Bible, people tell me that my programs are not really Christian."

Will they be effective at anything? Certainly not in their professions or occupations, because they lack the inner motivation. And certainly not in advancing the Kingdom of God here on earth, because they don't see the connection.

Meantime, Jesus Christ came in the flesh in order to show us that this earth is important. And He prayed for the Kingdom to come, on earth as it is in Heaven.

When lawyers defend the powerless and work for justice, they are doing God's work. When economists help foster a prosperous environment, they are doing God's work. When government officials help establish order and preserve freedom, they are doing God's work. When parents raise the next generation, they are doing God's work. And yes, the media does not have to be explicitly religious to serve God's purposes.

God is not just the head of the church. God is the head of the family, the justice system, the arts, politics, media, academia, and every other realm. He rules overall and wants the whole creation to reflect His glory.

Psalm 24:1-2
The earth is the Lord's, and everything in it, the world, and all who live in it; for he founded it on the seas and established it on the waters. NIV

From One-Dimensional to a Multi-Dimensional Life

Here we are on earth. We are Christians and want to please God and be responsible with what He has entrusted to us.

We have a family, work, attend church, live in a nation, need leisure/self-renewal time, and sometimes require further education.

But, how can we be faithful in all these areas of life? How do we succeed in all these jurisdictions or dimensions? How do we handle the many pressures and demands on our lives?

Should we devise a hierarchy of priorities for our different spheres of life and take care of one at the expense or in lieu of another?

It is a fact that we only have a limited amount of time -- 16 hours a day (besides sleeping) and 70-90 years of life-time. Our energy and finances are also limited, though usually in high demand.

And we want to be like Jesus. We want to be faithful, loyal, hardworking, and take care of everything entrusted to us. But how can we do that?

Our family wants (or so it seems) all our attention, energy, and finances. Our workplace, with its increasing demands and never ending projects, threatens to consume more and more of our time. Moreover, we feel that we are never doing enough with our church, helping with its many activities, good causes, Sunday school needs, and so on.

Our nation (including state and local levels) demands more and more of our finances (thus energy, and time) through taxation. We need exercise and self-renewal, and if we are attending school, forget it, life can become synonymous with the library.

In the midst of this frenzy, should we just neglect our family for the sake of our studies? Or justify our lack of commitment to our church because of work-related projects that need to be completed even on Sunday? Or, should we risk illness (including obesity) and even premature death because we do not find the time to exercise?

The fact is, we need a multi-dimensional life. A balance among all those apparently competing spheres of life. We need to take care of them all. Yes! But not in our own strength, or we blow up. We are not that good. We need God's grace. And God's wisdom. And God's power to do it all.

Galatians 5:25
If we are living now by the Holy Spirit's power, let us follow the Holy Spirit's leading in every part of our lives. TLB

From Our Timing to His Timing

It is true that, after the Fall, the relationship of humans with God deteriorated ostensibly. And even the Atonement of our Lord Jesus Christ did not completely restore that relationship.

This is so because though our spirit has been made alive again, we still live in corruptible bodies. We will only attain full intimacy with God when we are transformed, in the "twinkling of an eye" and join Him to live with Him forever.

Still, Scripture indicates that before the Fall a very close communion between God and Adam and Eve existed, and Adam and Eve were here on earth.

The sole fact that God would impose such stiff penalties on the human race, including death and hell, demonstrates that their act of disobedience (sin) had broken something precious and invaluable -- their close and intimate relationship with God.

Later on, in His mercy God decided to send Jesus Christ, His Son, to redeem the human race. That happened about 2,000 years ago.

Now, if we are going to believe that God's only intention is really to bring us all (His people) with Him to Heaven and get rid of the rest of the universe (roll it back), why did He not do it shortly after Jesus Christ came to earth?

There were many people then who put their trust in Him. Some may say that it is "because the world was not fully evangelized yet." And that may be true.

After all Scripture does say that "this gospel of the kingdom shall be preached in the whole world for a witness to all nations, and then the end shall come" (Mt.24: 14, NAS).

I have heard evangelists say, based on the latter, that we must all evangelize so we can "hurry up the return of the King."

Are we overlooking the fact that God, though interested in the evangelization of the world, is also a sovereign God?

Colossians 1:16-17

For in him all things were created: things in heaven and on earth, visible and invisible, whether thrones or powers or rulers or authorities; all things have been created through him and for him. He is before all things, and in him all things hold together.   NIV

From Mediocrity to Excellent Carpenter

As we contemplate our reduced and limited environment, product of our Christian glass ceilings, we feel exhausted, cramped, and uneasy about staying any longer here on earth. We want to soar, but in Heaven. We think there is no more room to soar here on earth, or in the different spheres of life (science, work, etc.), or in our minds or bodies.

As we wait for final passage into Heaven, once in a while we look up through the glass ceiling and see brief glimpses of other horizons, other realities, other frontiers to explore in our minds, in the arts, in outer space.

But since, according to our theology, those frontiers are not important, or relevant, or transcendent we just quickly look the other way, and suppress any excitement, attraction (which is even considered "temptation"), or motivation in exploring them.

Heaven is sufficient, is fast approaching, and is all there is to our existence.

What would our Lord Jesus Christ have said or done in this situation? Let us consider for a moment Jesus, the carpenter. A client approaches Jesus and requests a table to be made. The price and time of delivery are agreed upon.

At the due time the client is presented with a rough, unvarnished, unstable table (one leg is shorter than the others). In response to the client's bewilderment Jesus provides this excuse: "Well, I have other more important and transcendent work to do. I have to read the Scriptures, and visit the temple. I have to prepare myself for my ministry. I do not have time to spend in such an unimportant thing as making a table."

Even a popular movie on "The Life of Christ" presents an interesting scene. Somebody approaches Joseph and asks: "is your son not helping you with your carpentry?" And Joseph responds "he has more important things to do."

Do you believe for a moment that Jesus Christ could have been a mediocre carpenter? Mediocrity not only implies doing an insufficient job, but cheating others. If we are mediocre we are cheating our Lord, our family, our client/employer, and ourselves.

Of course, the Lord must have made the best tables, and must have had the integrity and honesty to give their clients what they requested (in this case a workable, good table) and their money's worth. In fact, John 20:7, talking about the resurrection, gives us a glimpse of Jesus's treatment of "ordinary things" when it states that the face-cloth, which had been on His head, [was found] not lying with the linen wrappings, but rolled up [folded] in a place by itself. (NAS).

That our Lord on His way back to Glory, after suffering and dying at the hands of humans, would take the time to fold this piece of cloth (there is no reason to believe that "it was the angels who did it") speaks volumes about the importance that the Lord placed on what some would consider "insignificant."

Daniel 6:3

Now Daniel so distinguished himself among the administrators and the satraps by his exceptional qualities that the king planned to set him over the whole kingdom. NIV

From Equal to More Equal than Others (The Family)

It is not excusable to neglect our children because we are working hard. It is not proper that because our pastor encouraged us to evangelize, we spend part of our office hours distributing tracts and "witnessing." It is not godly to overspend on our family and then not have enough for our church tithe.

Some may reason that some of these spheres or dimensions are more important, or more "transcendent" than the others and thus deserve a higher priority.

They usually see them as a pyramid, with God at the top, directly underneath comes the family or church, and then the rest. Others see them as different circles of life with the church circle on top of all others, and beneath disconnected circles for family, work, etc.

The fact is that God established all these jurisdictions of life, and therefore they must all have equal value. Concerning the state, there are abundant references in the Old Testament on why God is interested in law and order, how he established judges, laws, and authorities.

Romans 13 in the New Testament gives legitimacy to military and political authorities. Our Lord Jesus Christ Himself did not reject the state, but simply defined what is legitimate to give to Caesar.

The church was established by Christ. The family has been in God's heart from the beginning. Work was commanded by God and carried out even in the Garden of Eden. Rest is so important that God Himself rested on the seventh day of creation, and "blessed the seventh day and made it holy, because on it he rested from all the work of creating that he had done" (Gen. 2:3, NIV).

And I do not think it necessary to document to what extent the Lord is interested in us learning and acquiring knowledge (and wisdom) about Him, ourselves, and His creation.

Education is so integral to our human nature that it pervades the whole Bible.

The only distinction I would make is concerning the family. Though I believe there is equality between the family and the other dimensions of life, there is a difference in quality because the family is more vulnerable to change.

That is, while it is possible to replace, without major consequences, individual church members (or even the pastor), or the president of the nation, or employees at work, etc., it is not as easy to replace members of the family. It is not that the father or mother is indispensable (only God is indispensable), but he or she is in fact irreplaceable.

The loss of one of the parents has significant and far reaching consequences on the other spouse, and certainly on the children. That is why, when juggling all these spheres (balls) of life in a beautiful balance, we must be especially careful when dealing with the family. As an acquaintance says, the latter is the "glass ball."

Psalm 128:3-4

Your wife will be like a fruitful vine within your house; your children will be like olive shoots around your table. Yes, this will be the blessing for the man who fears the Lord. NIV

From Witnessing to Embodying Jesus

Why should homemakers, politicians, plumbers, students and the like, being the overwhelming majority of the Christian church, have to desperately "glean" a little here and a little there from messages and books that, written and delivered by pastors, are directed (consciously or unconsciously) to actual or would-be pastors, evangelists, and missionaries?

On the other hand, non-Christians are in fact interested in spiritual matters. Just look at the explosive growth of people calling themselves "spiritual," new-age groups and other religious organizations.

While it is true that non-believers are mainly interested in a spirituality and gods that they can dominate, control, and use at their discretion (as do some believers), there is a growing sense that those man-made gods are not sufficient to satisfy people's deepest spiritual longings.

Everyone desperately needs the reality of Jesus Christ in their lives.

There was a missionary doctor among a tribal group. He used to nurse an old widow very poor and ill, while witnessing to her. Since the lady did not understand the concepts about Jesus Christ and his salvation, she one day asked "Please, explain to me more clearly what this Jesus is like."

In a moment of "high inspiration" the missionary answered, "Jesus is like me!" To which the woman replied in excitement, "Oh, if Jesus is like you, then I love Him, too, for He is so good!"

Mind boggling? Maybe. But, aren't we God's physical expression here on earth? Aren't we His ambassadors? Have we not been purposed to conform to His image?

The problem may be that we have been too religious, or too preachy in addressing society with the Christian message. We need to live the Gospel, more than just speaking it.

For, if speaking the message were enough, wouldn't we have evangelized the world in 2,000 plus years? Not only is most of the world not yet evangelized, but Christianity is even shrinking in supposedly "Christian" regions such as the United States and Europe.

People of other religions will not be attracted to Christ by "hearing" the message preached, but by witnessing Christ in us.

Galatians 5:13
You, my brothers and sisters, were called to be free. But do not use your freedom to indulge the flesh; rather, serve one another humbly in love. NIV

From Time-Constrained to the Fullness of Time

We also need a horizontal-spatial inter-connection. The development of science and technology requires a strong and reliable political system, a prosperous economy, a legal system that encourages and protects invention and creativity, a strong work ethic, a long-term vision and commitment, high educational levels, and the national will to undertake larger-than-life projects.

A short-term vision of the world would never have accomplished any of this. In fact, if our forefathers and foremothers had had this short-term mentality, the whole American experiment with its contributions to the world in terms of constitutional principles, a missionary effort, financial aid, technological progress, etc. would never have taken place.

Not only that, but to insist on a theology that despises science, technology, the arts, etc. (though in practice we all gladly make use of these) is to declare that the American experiment is but a waste.

And of course, this kind of mentality is not limited only to Christians. There are now strong efforts at the United Nations level, with the active participation of the United States government, to limit industrial development by limiting the release of chemicals and other contaminants into the air.

As an internationally recognized leader of this movement has implied, the ideal is to give up driving cars and ride bicycles instead. Which is what we would be doing (only it wouldn't be bicycles but horses) if those that came before us had adopted the "evangelization only" mentality.

Reality is far different. We must live the gospel, not just preach it, if we want to transform our world (evangelism in the broader sense) and even if we want to evangelize the people of this world (in the narrow sense).

Research published by The Barna Report demonstrates that "evangelism through personal relationships produces almost twice as many converts as do sermons, church services, and evangelistic events."

It is our lives, lived in the fullness of our humanness that will ultimately accomplish the transformation of this world and will point people to Christ. Or as Francis D'Asissi would say "preach the Gospel at all times, if need be use words."

What must we do then? I believe it is high time to shatter the Christian glass ceiling, at the individual, collective, and global levels, and reach for Christ's ceiling. Christ's ceiling encompasses spirit, body, and mind; it is big enough for church, work, family, science, and the arts; it is magnificent enough to include the Earth, the Moon, Pluto, the Milky Way, and other galaxies -- indeed the whole universe!

And a last thought: if God were not really interested in the body, the earth, etc., why would He have promised to give us new and incorruptible bodies? And why would He want to create "new heavens and a new earth"? (2 Pet. 3:13, Rev. 21:1, NAS).

Could this new wine, new heaven, new earth, and all things new, be related to the Feast of the Lamb and His Bride (the Church), that will go on forever and ever, from glory to glory and magnificence to magnificence?

Isaiah 6:3
And they were calling to one another: "Holy, holy, holy is the Lord Almighty; the whole earth is full of his glory."
NIV

About the Author:

With my wonderful wife Rael

I'm an artist at heart. And yes, I have been an artist all my life. And of course, I've always loved feasts, and especially a feast of blessings!

My first painting, Boys by the Lake, in oils, dates back to middle school, and it illustrates the back cover of my previous book, Resurrection in the Valley of the Shadow of Death, available on Amazon https://www.amazon.com/-/es/Pedro-C-Moreno/dp/B08ZDGRD75

Two of my paintings are on the front and back covers of this book. My daily occupation is as an executive. Some years ago I saw a friend I admire in North Carolina and found out he had been doing watercolors. So, I just got started with watercolors, and now I also do acrylics, especially when I'm relaxing at home at night, or on weekends. Over 500 of my paintings are now with friends, family and others all over the United States and in 15 other countries.

I give the original paintings away as a gift. Through my painting, poetry and books, I want to show you that God loves you unconditionally and wants to be very close to you. In terms of my painting style, I humbly feel I belong to the stenographic school (Raoul Dufy and the like), with a minimalist approach and leaving much of the perception of the work to the viewer. I was inspired by Degas, who was going blind and decided to paint an "orgy of colors," that is bright, optimistic, full of life. It develops my emotional intelligence!

Over the years I have worked as an author, executive, speaker and consultant on health and social policy. I have served in the private sector as well as the Federal and State governments, managing large institutions, and serving persons with disabilities, mental health and substance abuse issues, helping kids get adopted in the U.S., promotion of girls education in India, working to help Veterans get treatment, training and employment, fighting trafficking in persons, supporting healthy families, combating illegal drug use among youth, facilitating the re-entry of ex-prisoners into society, helping with refugee resettlement, working for religious and ethnic reconciliation, and generally helping marginalized and low income individuals and communities get mainstreamed.

In addition to a Law Degree from the University of San Andrés in La Paz, Bolivia, I was blessed to receive a Master's of Arts in international law and economic development from The Fletcher School of Law and Diplomacy at Tufts University and to complete the Specialization in Negotiation and Dispute Resolution at

Harvard University. I've had the privilege of traveling in 68 countries on all continents, where I take advantage to practice my Spanish and French.

To learn more about Penta Global, which is the ministry Rael and I are doing together in order to attract people to the Feast of Blessings, and bring you peace with God, peace with yourself, and peace with others, and become a partner in mission with us, go here:
https://thecause.kindful.com/?campaign=1179954

To see some of my paintings, which are on the Saatchi Art website, go to this link:
https://www.saatchiart.com/account/artworks/1143265

I would love to hear from you and your feedback on this book. Please e-mail me at: PedroCMoreno7@gmail.com

Made in the USA
Columbia, SC
18 July 2023

20248971R00124